MW00333665

7REALITIES
THE DEVIL
DOESN'T WANT YOU TO KNOW

Covenant Truths For Daily Living

—— MICHAEL ATUNRASE, SR ——

7REALITIES
THE DEVIL
DOESN'T WANT YOU TO KNOW

Covenant Truths For Daily Living

——— MICHAEL ATUNRASE, SR ———

PRAISE FOR 7 REALITIES THE DEVIL DOESN'T WANT YOU TO KNOW

On the title of the book... 7 REALITIES THE DEVIL DOESN'T WANT YOU TO KNOW. The title of the book is not only Biblically/theologically sound, but is also fresh and contemporary. It is very relevant in this church era. Religious pluralism, secularism, renewed increase in new age movement and cold church orthodoxy affect how believers view the personality and works of Satan. The title is plain and declarative. No novelty and gimmick.

On the language style of the book... The author has intended to reach ALL and therefore uses a popular and non-technical language that is easy to comprehend the truths of the book and be inspired to apply them to daily living.

On the examples utilized in this book... The examples and quotes used in the book are well chosen to provide clear illustration to reinforce the principles discussed in the book.

The good balance presented in this book ... Many works on this subject have failed to present the real tension or the balance found in the Bible concerning afflictions in the Christian life. While some well-meaning believers attribute all afflictions or trials as coming from Satan, others on the opposite extreme seem to glorify afflictions and trials as coming from God and as marks of faithfulness for obedient Saints of God. This books strongly affirms what it presents here but does not indiscriminately see ALL afflictions as evil.

On how the topics are presented in the book... This book is based on the first chapter of the book of Exodus and discusses each topic in a coherent, logical sequence. The first part provides foundational contexts on which the 7 Covenant Realities are built upon. The natural and intelligent progression of discussion from the first covenant reality to the final one is excellent so that one truth leads to another.

The uniqueness of the book... The recap at the end of each chapter provides a powerful summary of each topic. It is like the author is saying, "You may forget all the details but do not forget these ones." The three levels or aspects of learning is presented as:

- **Reality- Biblical**
- **Truth-Theological**
- **YOU-Practical/personal**

It is the final level that the cognitive knowledge is translated to personal application resulting in personal transformation.

Dr. Jerry M. Pescoy, Senior Pastor
Christian City Church-Agape, Baguio, Philippines

Copyright © 2016 by Michael Atunrase, Sr.

All rights reserved. Printed in the United States of America. No part of this book may be used or reproduced in any manner whatsoever without written permission except in the case of brief quotations embodied in critical articles or reviews.

Unless otherwise specified, all Scripture quotations are taken from *The Holy Bible*, New King James Version NKJV, copyright © 1982 by Thomas Nelson, Inc. Used by permission. All rights reserved.

Scripture quotations marked NIV are taken from *The Holy Bible*, New International Version, ®NIV®, copyright © 1973, 1978, 1984 by Biblica, Inc.™ Used by permission of Zondervan. All rights reserved worldwide.

Scripture quotations marked AMP are taken from the Amplified Bible, Copyright © 1954, 1958, 1962, 1964, 1965, 1987 by The Lockman Foundation. Used by permission.

Scripture quotations marked NLT are taken from *The Holy Bible*, New Living Translation, copyright © 1996, 2004, 2007, by Tyndale House Foundation. Used by permission of Tyndale House Publishers, Inc., Carol Stream, Illinois 60188. All rights reserved.

Scripture quotations marked MSG are taken from *The Holy Bible*, The Message (MSG), Copyright © 1993, 1994, 1995, 1996, 2000, 2001, 2002 by Eugene H. Peterson

Scripture quotations marked BSB are taken from *The Holy Bible*, Berean Study Bible, (BSB) Copyright ©2016 by Bible Hub Used by Permission. All Rights Reserved Worldwide.

Scriptures marked KJV are taken from the King James Version (KJV): KING JAMES VERSION, public domain.

Scripture quotations marked Weymouth are from the Weymouth New Testament, Richard Francis Weymouth, 1912. Public domain in the United States.

ISBN: 0978-0997520002

For information contact; address

MOLAT PUBLISHERS

P. O. Box 82, Morrisville, PA 19067

DEDICATION

*To my loving wife Lola, thank you for the
sacrifices you have made to allow me to
pursue the call of God upon my life.
To Michael Jr., Emily-Rachael,
Sarah-Elizabeth and Joshua-Emmanuel,
our beloved children,
I thank you all for your love and support.
To all the children the Lord has given
us around the world; the Lord has
enlarged our borders through you.
To all my friends in ministry at home and overseas,
your friendship has made me better.
To the Body of Christ, may the truths learned
from this book bring about a revolution in
your lives to the glory of God.*

FOREWORD

Dr. Atunrase has CRAFTED a master study guide that all believers should possess commensurate with the timing of their New Life. To have learned this compact teaching and the valuable lessons this book offers would have saved me a lot of heartache as a young believer. I don't think you could add anything to this composite teaching...it is a "stand alone", a must to all who can hardly grasp suffering and troubles as Christians.

The basic usage of Israel as God's example to perpetuate His eternal principles and purposes, clearly illustrates and translates today to His Church. It is clear that this subject is amplified by the Holy Spirt to the author, as he has also laid it out for the body of Christ.

This teaching is timeless as is His Word! My spirit rejoices that this book will be invaluable to many, for years to come. I ask for permission to quote you on many of your anointed, well-arranged, and thought-out teachings.

Bishop Lynn Burling
PRESIDENT, FROM THE HEART MINISTRIES
SENIOR PASTOR, CHRISTIAN FAITH CHURCH
BELVILLE, TEXAS

TABLE OF CONTENTS

Preface   9
Introduction   10
PART 1   14

CHAPTER 1
The Reality of Your Redemptive Provisions
and Covenant Rights 32

CHAPTER 2
The Reality of the Superiority
of Your Covenant Status 40

CHAPTER 3
The Reality of Your Spiritual Potential................................. 52

CHAPTER 4
The Reality of the Source of All Spiritual Warfare
and Afflictions.. 69

CHAPTER 5
The Reality of the Benefits of Trials 77

CHAPTER 6
The Reality of the Remarkable Impact of a Christ-like Life....... 90

CHAPTER 7
The Reality of Divine Favor on Your life 104

Scripture Index   125
About the Author   129
Notes   132

ACKNOWLEDGEMENTS

I want to acknowledge and thank the One, who raised a little boy of ten years from the grave, and made him a Kingdom Servant, to Him be all the glory......the Lord Jesus Christ.

I want to thank my number one fan, Lola, my extraordinary wife, the one who always has stood by me and made great sacrifices for me to pursue God's call. I couldn't have come this far without you.

Thank you to my wonderful children, Michael Jr., Emily-Rachael, Sarah-Elizabeth and Joshua-Emmanuel, fellow laborers in the Kingdom. I am grateful for you, your love for the Lord inspires me. Thank you Mom Elizabeth, for your prayers and support.

Thank you to Rev. Lonnie and Nathalie Reed, Dr. Henry Harbuck, Dr. Charles Henderson, Pastors Samuel and Bernice Abegunde, for your many years of leadership and example of faithfulness in ministry.

Thank you to Pastors Lynn and Linda Burling, Pastors K. V. and Lily Daniel, for your love and friendship through the years.

Thank you to Dr. Elizabeth Kennedy, and Pastors Gary and Carol Hall, for encouraging me to write this book.

Thank you to Dr. Jerry Pescoy for your excellent review and wonderful comments about this book.

Thank you to Min. Carol Di Santo for your excellent editorial assistance, and thank you to Jordan Lollis for your help editing part of this book.

Thank you to Pastor Mahi Pal Singh for your prayers throughout the period of writing this book.

Thanks to many members of Association of Evangelical Gospel Assemblies, my friends and colleagues, the International Council of Bishops your friendships is invaluable.

I am also grateful for the many members, friends and ministry staff at Cornerstone Bible Fellowship Church, whose faithfulness, constant prayers and support, inspire me to continue to be the best God wants me to be.

PREFACE

Exodus is called the Book of Redemption. The book furnishes us with some of the most important themes in Biblical Theology: Election, Redemption, Salvation, Worship, Law, Covenant and Priesthood. The Exodus experience is to the Old Testament, what the cross of Christ is to Christianity. In Exodus, we see the redemptive act of God in saving His people Israel from Pharaoh and Egypt's bondage. Likewise, in the New Testament, we see God's redemptive act through Christ to deliver his people from Satan and Sin. The life of Israel is like that of the Christian Church in an extrapolated sense; and on a personal level, like the life of the individual believer in the world.

In this book, I have attempted to share Covenant Truths gleaned from a study of the first chapter of the book of Exodus. The subject of Redemptive Provisions is a vast one and not limited to these seven topics, but for the purpose of this book, these truths are unearthed to picture the believer's life in the world (Egypt), the Devil (the Pharaohs of this world) and the Devil's machinations (Spiritual warfare and strategies) against the believer in the world.

Abundant Life is experienced as one hears and then puts into practice the Word of God. Jesus emphasized this point that the blessing is in the doing (practice). Jesus replied, *"But even more blessed are all who hear the word of God and put it into practice"* (Luke 11:28 New Living Translation). Also, He said, *"Now that you know these things, God will bless you for doing them"* (John 13:17 NLT).

The point of this book therefore, is to encourage the believer to adopt these Old Testament truths for daily living by making practical everyday decisions to walk in these covenant realities. For **the believer** to realize the Abundant Life (John 10:10), he **must be a practitioner**. Practicing the Word of God is a proven covenant technique for victorious living. I believe you are on your way to Living Abundantly and fulfilling your covenant destiny.

Dr. Michael Atunrase, Sr.

INTRODUCTION

As you read this book, you will encounter some truths that will change the way you live your life. Unless you have knowledge about something, you cannot imagine or desire it, because you cannot desire what you don't know. Knowledge initiates desire and desire creates imagination; imagination is the picture of things desired. In the same way, spiritual knowledge acquaints you with divine provisions (what God has provided) and spiritual understanding (revelation) shows you how to obtain them.

The Advantage of Spiritual Understanding

"..... It is not good for a person to be without knowledge...." **(Proverbs 19:2 Amplified Bible).**

The moment you are aware of what Jesus can do for you, at that moment, you are able to change your life or your circumstances, if you respond to the truth you have encountered. Spiritual understanding is key to personal or city transformations. A whole region was radically impacted because some of the people in the city knew what Jesus could do for them. They welcomed His presence and took advantage of the power available to them.

*"And **when the men of that place recognized Him**, they sent out into all that surrounding region, brought to Him all who were sick"* **(Matthew 14:35).**

The moment the Samaritan woman understood what Jesus could do for her, she responded and said, *"Sir, give me this water"* (John 4:15). Also some of the five thousand people, that were fed by Jesus in the wilderness asked Him, *"Lord evermore, give us this bread"* **(John 6:34 KJV)**. God has provided many things for you in Christ in order to maximize your life here on earth. It will take spiritual understanding for you to access them.

> *"And we have received God's Spirit (not the world's spirit),* **so we can know the wonderful things God has freely given us"** **(1 Corinthians 2:12 NLT)**.

You will also ask God for the things He has provided for you, the moment you are aware of them, and understand you can have them.

The Power of Knowledge

Without knowledge, there is no possessing your covenant blessings. It is your spiritual understanding that determines the quality of your life on earth. Knowledge opens the door to a world of possibilities; whereas ignorance is being trapped behind a closed door.

It is your spiritual understanding that determines the quality of your life on earth.

"A giant ship engine failed. The ship's owners tried one expert after another, but none of them could figure how to fix the engine. Then they brought in an old man who had been fixing ships since he was a young man. He carried a large bag of tools with him, and when he arrived, he immediately went to work. He inspected the engine very carefully, top to bottom. Two of the ship's owners were there, watching this man, hoping he would know what to do. After looking things over, the old man reached into his bag and pulled out a small hammer. He gently tapped

11

something. Instantly, the engine lurched into life. He carefully put his hammer away. The engine was fixed! A week later, the owners received a bill from the old man for ten thousand dollars. 'What?!' the owners exclaimed. 'He hardly did anything!' So they wrote the old man a note saying, 'Please send us an itemized bill.' "
The man sent a bill that read:

Tapping with a hammer:	$2.00
Knowing where to tap:	$ 9,998.00
	$ 10,000.00

-Author unknown.

The Tragedy of Spiritual Ignorance

The Bible is filled with lessons about the consequences of spiritual ignorance. Throughout the Bible, we are admonished to increase in spiritual knowledge. God's very heart cry for His people has always been about their spiritual ignorance.

"My people are destroyed for lack of knowledge..." **(Hosea 4:6a).**

"Therefore My people have gone into captivity, because they have no knowledge; Their honorable men are famished, and their multitude dried up with thirst" **(Isaiah 5:13).**

Ignorance is no bliss! Its consequence has often proven fatal. The Apostle Paul in his letter to the Corinthian Church warned them against spiritual ignorance. He wanted them to know that spiritual ignorance will make them victims of the enemy. Satan is an opportunist; he takes advantage of people's ignorance. You have heard people say, 'what you don't know cannot kill you' but that is not true. What you don't know is already killing you. Satan feeds on people's ignorance.

> *"Lest Satan should take advantage of us: for we are not ignorant of his devices"* **(2 Corinthians 2:11)**.

There are myriads of people who will die without discovering or knowing the love of God, or never experience all that God has provided for them in Jesus. Jesus spoke these words as he grieved over the people and the city of Jerusalem.

> *"If you had only known today what could have brought you peace! But now it is hidden from your sight"* **(Luke 19:42 International Standard Version[1]).**

Apostle Paul prayed for the Ephesian Christians, that they may come to know their good fortunes and covenant destiny in Christ; a prayer to know the hope to which they were called, and the glorious inheritance reserved for those who are in Christ, how wonderful!

> *"the eyes of your understanding being enlightened; that you may know what is the hope of His calling, what are the riches of the glory of His inheritance in the saints"* **(Ephesians 1:18)**.

PART 1

The children of Israel had a comfortable existence in Egypt; until some years after the death of Joseph. Life in Goshen was pleasant, and with the blessings of increase in population, comes the abundant supply for their livelihood and sustenance.

*"Now **the Israelites settled in Egypt** in the region of Goshen. They acquired property there **and were fruitful and increased greatly in number"* **(Genesis 47:27 New International Version).**

*"⁷**But the children of Israel were fruitful and increased abundantly, multiplied and grew exceedingly mighty; and the land was filled with them.** ⁸Now there arose a new king over Egypt, who did not know Joseph. ⁹And he said to his people, "Look, the people of the children of Israel are more and mightier than we; ¹⁰come, let us deal shrewdly with them, lest they multiply, and it happen, in the event of war, that they also join our enemies and fight against us, and so go up out of the land"* **(Exodus 1:7-10).**

A New King Arose

The Israelites continue to multiply until Goshen became the envy of all the provinces of Egypt, with the largest revenue. Afterwards a new king became Pharaoh, who did not know Joseph, or all that he did for the land of Egypt. In the meantime, the Hebrews had grown into such alarming numbers, and this of course became a great concern for the new king. The new king was not only grappling with the population explosion; but the increasing influence of an alien people, and the possibilities of future rebellion.

Pharaoh's Evil Policy

In order to curtail what he deemed a threat to his kingdom. Pharaoh came up with an evil scheme, aimed directly at controlling Israel's posterity. He supposed that by enslaving them and forcing them into a life of hard labor, he would be able to diminish their physical strength, depress their spirits, and subdue them mentally and consequently affect their reproduction.

It is a proven fact that, forced labor, mistreatments, starvation and inhuman conditions, have been effective tools for subduing a people mentally and physically. It is surprising to note however, that Pharaoh's policy backfired, and the very things he feared happened. *"No weapon formed against you (Israel) shall prosper"* (**Isaiah 54:17**).

The Promise of Posterity

But how did Israel grow to be so many? What was responsible for this increase in population? Who could have thought that a band of seventy plus people, could come into a nation and in a couple of hundred years increased to such multitude, as to become a threat to their host nation? For it was obvious that Israel had increased at a rate beyond the human process. The answer is traceable only to divine intervention. The scriptures noted the following:

> *"As **the time drew near** for **God to fulfill his promise to Abraham, the number of our people in Egypt had greatly increased"* (**Acts 7:17 NIV**).

"The LORD made his people very fruitful; **he made them too numerous for their foes"** (Psalm 105:24 NIV).

"David did not take the number of the men twenty years old or less, because **the LORD had promised to make Israel as numerous as the stars in the sky"** (1 Chronicles 27:23 NIV).

God made these promises time and time again, first to Abraham; then to Isaac and then to Jacob.

To Abraham:

*"***I will make you into a great nation***, and I will bless you; I will make your name great, and you will be a blessing"* **(Genesis 12:2 NIV).**

"Then He brought him outside and said, "Look now toward heaven, and count the stars if you are able to number them." And He said to him, "So shall your descendants be" **(Genesis 15:5).**

To Isaac:

*"³.... **I will perform the oath which I swore to Abraham your father.**⁴And I will make your descendants multiply as the stars of heaven; I will give to your descendants all these lands; and in your seed all the nations of the earth shall be blessed"* **(Genesis 26:3-4).**

To Jacob:

*"I am God, the God of your father," he said. "**Do not be afraid to go down to Egypt, for I will make***

you into a great nation there" **(Genesis 46:3 NIV).**

*"..... ³**God Almighty appeared to me** at Luz in the land of Canaan, and there He blessed me, ⁴**and said to me, 'I am going to make you fruitful and increase your numbers**. I will make you a community of peoples, and I will give this land as an everlasting possession to your descendants after you"* **(Genesis 48:3-4 NIV).**

It is clear from scriptures then, that the reason for this unusual growth in population was because God promised it. He promised to make them numerous. This promise from God was to be the picture of their future (covenant destiny). And it was the fulfilment of this promise that became the enemy's contention. The enemy will always react to the manifestations or the fulfilment of God's promises in your life. You can be sure that the Devil

> *The enemy will always react to the manifestations or the fulfilment of God's promises in your life....*

will launch his attacks at certain seasons of your life, and one of those times will be at a time of fulfilling destiny.
The devil will come up with a thousand ways to frustrate the promises of God to you, and try all means to resist your rising.

The blessings of God on the children of Israel became a visible threat for their enemy. They woke up one day and find themselves enslaved and in bondage to Pharaoh. They will not know why they suddenly lost their freedom; neither will they know that their suffering was as a result of the manifestation of their covenant blessings.

If they knew what their enemy knows about them, it might have changed their behavior and strengthened their courage. If we know the truths the enemy knows about us, we will not lose courage during the conflict, but rather be fearless and confident in our resolve to resist his schemes. As A. R.

> *If we know the truths the enemy knows about us, we will not lose courage during the conflict, but rather be fearless and confident in our resolve to resist his schemes.*

Bernard, said, *"The ignorance of the oppressed is strength for the oppressor."*

> *"Therefore* **My people have gone into captivity, because they have no knowledge;** *Their honorable men are famished, and their multitude dried up with thirst"* **(Isaiah 5:13).**

The Devil's Attack is Based on Prior Knowledge

The Devil is not all-knowing, but all of his attacks on people are based on prior-knowledge, or acquaintance with some facts about the person. The Devil said to God concerning Job,

> *"…. ⁹Does Job fear God for nothing? ¹⁰Have You not made a hedge around him, around his household, and around all that he has on every side? You have blessed the work of his hands, and his possessions have increased in the land"* **(Job 1:9-10).**

The Devil said, there was a hedge around Job (personally), around his household (family), and all that he had (properties, including his servants), and also that, God's blessing is upon his work and had made Job to become successful and enviable in the land. It is interesting to note that, the Devil would disclose this. It would be quite impossible for you to know that I have a fence or hedge around my house, unless you had first visited me. In other words, the Devil was implying that he had tried Job before now, but could not get to Job or prevail against him because there was a fence, a hedge of protection around him.

"The angel of the Lord encamps all around those who fear Him, and delivers them" **(Psalm 34:7).**

Understanding the Meaning of Redemption in the Old Testament

The word redemption is used in several ways in the Old Testament, and all of the usages gives us a full picture of the comprehensive nature of the word. The basic meaning is to 'buy back'. The word is used in:

Rescuing from Dangers

*"The Angel who has **redeemed me from all evil**, Bless the lads; Let my name be named upon them, and the name of my fathers Abraham and Isaac; And let them grow into a multitude in the midst of the earth"* **(Genesis 48:16).**

Deliverance from Bondage

*"Therefore say to the children of Israel: 'I am the Lord; **I will bring you out** from under the burdens of the Egyptians, **I will rescue you** from their bondage, and*

I will redeem you with an outstretched arm and with great judgments" **(Exodus 6:6).**

Release from Servitude

"⁴⁷Now if a sojourner or stranger close to you becomes rich, and one of your brethren who dwells by him becomes poor, and sells himself to the stranger or sojourner close to you, or to a member of the stranger's family,⁴⁸after he is sold he may be redeemed again. One of his brothers may redeem him; ⁴⁹or his uncle or his uncle's son may redeem him; or anyone who is near of kin to him in his family may redeem him; or if he is able he may redeem himself" **(Leviticus 25:47-49).**

Restoring Family's Fortunes

"If one of your fellow Israelites becomes poor and sells some of their property, their nearest relative is to come and redeem what they have sold" **(Leviticus 25:25 NIV).**

"³Then he said to the close relative, "Naomi, who has come back from the country of Moab, sold the piece of land which belonged to our brother Elimelech.⁴And I thought to inform you, saying, 'Buy it back in the presence of the inhabitants and the elders of my people. If you will redeem it, redeem it; but if you will not redeem it, then tell me, that I may know; for there is no one but you to redeem it, and I am next after you. 'And he said, I will redeem it" **(Ruth 4:3-4).**

Redemption is a trade word; it is the price paid to buy something or someone back. To redeem is to purchase back at a cost. We belong to God because we are His creation, but became separated from Him through Adam's sin. Now *'the wages of sin is death'* (Romans 6:23), we owed a debt we could not pay. God therefore offered His Son to die (to pay the debt) in our place. And through the shedding of His precious blood, Jesus redeemed us back to God, from the slave market of sin. Christ's death satisfied all the legal demand for our freedom.

The New Testament Interpretation of Redemption

The meaning is preserved in the New Testament, only more explicit. Consider these scriptures:

> **"Who gave himself for us, that he might redeem us from all iniquity,** and purify unto himself a peculiar people, zealous of good works" **(Titus 2:14 KJV).**

> "But **we were hoping that it was He who was going to redeem Israel.** Indeed, besides all this, today is the third day since these things happened" **(Luke 24:21).**

> "[18]Knowing that **you were not redeemed with corruptible things,** like silver or gold, from your aimless conduct received by tradition from your fathers, [19]**but with the precious blood of Christ**, as of a lamb without blemish and without spot" **(1 Peter 1:18-19)**.

The word here translated 'redeemed' is the Greek word *lutroo*; which means to liberate by payment of ransom; or to deliver from evils of every kind, internal and external, as these two disciples expressed on the way to Emmaus, of their hope of Jesus as the One, to have delivered Israel from Rome's captivity.

This word '*lutroo*' was also used in another way, which portrays a benefactor going to the slave market, for the sole purpose of purchasing slaves out of slavery to liberate and set them free. The payment is called a *ransom*. The word *lutroo* distinctly pictured the shedding of Jesus' blood as ransom for our permanent deliverance and freedom from satanic powers that once held us captive.

> "*Neither by the blood of goats and calves, but by his own blood, He entered in once into the holy place, having obtained **eternal redemption for us**" (Hebrews 9:12 KJV).*

Out of the Slave Market

> "**Christ has redeemed us from the curse of the law**, *having become a curse for us (for it is written, "Cursed is everyone who hangs on a tree")" (Galatians 3:13).*

In this verse, the Apostle employed a very interesting Greek word, '*exagoridzo*', a compound of the words *ex* and *agoridzo*. The word *ex* means out, as in Exodus or Exit, and the word agoridzo was the Greek word most commonly used to depict the slave market.

Again the word graphically detailed that of a ***buyer-redeemer,*** who paid a high price to recover a slave from the custody of another (paying off), **in order to bring him out of captivity to permanent freedom.**

*"⁴But when the fullness of the time was come, **God sent forth his Son**, made of a woman, made under the law, ⁵to **redeem** them that were under the law, **that we might receive the adoption of sons"***
(Galatians 4:4-5 KJV).

Understanding the Meaning of Salvation in the Old Testament

The word translated *saved*, and *saving* in theses verses is the Hebrew word, '*yasha*' means to deliver; to preserve, and to rescue.

Israel in Egypt

*"Thus **the LORD saved Israel that day** out of the hand of the Egyptians; and Israel saw the Egyptians dead on the sea shore"* **(Exodus 14:30 KJV).**

*"Then Jonathan said to the young man who bore his armor, 'Come, let us go over to the garrison of these uncircumcised; it may be that the Lord will work for us. For **nothing restrains the Lord from saving** by many or by few.'"* **(1 Samuel 14:6).**

*"Look unto me and be **saved**, all you end of the earth ..."* **(Isaiah 45:22).**

Does Redemption and Salvation Mean the Same Thing?

Actually redemption is the first step in our Salvation. Redemption is the payment by God for the sins of humanity, through the death of Christ on the cross. Redemption is for all, because Christ died for everyman. The scriptures say,

> *"⁵For there is one God and **one Mediator between God and men, the Man Christ Jesus, ⁶who gave Himself a ransom for all,"** (1 Timothy 2:5-6).*

Christ died for everyman, *'a ransom for all'*. This is the case for the Great commission; we must go and tell everyone, everywhere that Christ, has redeemed them to God.

All Men Are Redeemed But Not All Men Are Saved

John 3:16, is the most frequently quoted verse of the Bible, but unfortunately also the most misunderstood verse of the Bible. This favorite scripture verse explains clearly the difference between redemption and salvation.

> *"For God so loved the world that He gave His only begotten Son, that whoever believes in Him should not perish but have everlasting life"* **(John 3:16).**

Notice it says, God so loved the world and gave His only begotten Son (for the redemption of **the world**, that is everyone), but the other part of the verse says, that **'whosoever'** (that is, anyone) who believes in Him (Christ) should not perish but have eternal life (Salvation).

Salvation Requires Faith in Jesus

While Redemption is universal and collective, salvation is the application of redemption to the individuals, salvation is personal. Redemption does not require personal belief, but to experience salvation one needs a personal belief and faith in Christ and His atoning work. It is those who believe in Jesus in the world that have eternal life (Salvation). The Apostles Peter and Paul explained this further:

All men are redeemed, but not all men are saved.

> *"To Him all the prophets witness that, through His name, **whoever believes in Him will receive remission of sins**" (Acts 10:43).*

> *"But the Scripture has confined all under sin, that **the promise** by faith in Jesus Christ **might be given to those who believe**" (Galatians 3:22).*

Salvation Includes Much More

Salvation includes much more than the forgiveness of sins; it leads to a much fuller experience. A man does not experience regeneration just because he knows Jesus died for

It is those who believe in Jesus in the world that have eternal life (Salvation).

him (redemption), but he experiences regeneration when he personally received Christ into his life and is saved by Christ (salvation).

Salvation Includes

Regeneration-The New Birth

Regeneration is the life of Christ in a believer, (the resurrected life), it is Christ likeness. The nature of holiness, is Christs' life imparted to the believer, and the fruit of salvation is the expression of the divine nature.

> *"For if while we were enemies **we were reconciled to God through the death of His Son,** it is much more [certain], now that we are reconciled, that we shall be saved (daily delivered from sin's dominion) through His (resurrection life)"* **(Romans 5:10 AMPC[2]).**

> *"By which have been **given to us** exceedingly great and precious promises, **that** through these **you may be partakers of the divine nature,** having escaped the corruption that is in the world through lust"* **(2 Peter 1:4).**

> *"That which is born of the flesh is flesh, and **that which is born of the Spirit is spirit"* (John 3:6).**

> *"But **now having been set free from sin,** and having become slaves of God, you have your fruit to holiness, and the end, everlasting life"* **(Romans 6:22).**

Transformation- A complete change from the old man

> *"Therefore, if anyone is in Christ, he is a new creation; old things have passed away; behold, **all things have become new"* (2 Corinthians 5:17).**

> *"And do not be conformed to this world, **but be transformed by the renewing of your mind,** that you may prove what is that good and acceptable and perfect will of God"* **(Romans 12:2).**

*"But we all, with unveiled face, beholding as in a mirror the glory of the Lord, **are being transformed** into the same image from glory to glory, just as by the Spirit of the Lord"* **(2 Corinthians 3:18).**

Justification-
Declared to be right and in good standing with God

Justification does not mean we were *'made right'* with God, but rather that we are declared by God, to be right with Himself. If we were made right, then we couldn't sin anymore.

"Therefore, as through one man's offense judgment came to all men, resulting in condemnation, even so through one Man's righteous act the free gift came to all men, resulting in justification of life" **(Romans 5:18).**

"Moreover whom He predestined, these He also called; whom He called, these He also justified; and whom He justified, these He also glorified" **(Romans 8:30).**

Fruitfulness- Producing the results of the New Life

*"You did not choose Me, but **I chose you** and appointed you **that you should go and bear fruit,** and that your fruit should remain, that whatever you ask the Father in My Name He may give you"* **(John 15:16).**

*"**The righteous shall flourish** like a palm tree, **He shall grow** like a cedar in Lebanon"* **(Psalm 92:12).**

Understanding the Meaning of Salvation in the New Testament

The word translated Salvation in the New Testament is the Greek word, *'Soteria'*, and it means deliverance; preservation, welfare, soundness, restoration, prosperity, safety and healing. And is the word used in all these scripture verses,

> "Nor is there **salvation** in any other, **for there is no other name under heaven** given among men **by which we must be saved**" (Acts 4:12).

> "And Jesus said to him, "Today **salvation has come to this house,** because he also is a son of Abraham;" (Luke 19:9).

Salvation is a Comprehensive Blessing

Since the word Salvation is comprehensive in its meaning, we can read the verse in **Acts 4:12**, as this,

> "Nor is there **salvation** (deliverance; preservation, welfare, soundness, restoration, prosperity, safety and healing), in any other **for there is no other name under heaven** given among men **by which we must be saved** (delivered; preserved, have-welfare, have-soundness, restored, prosper, safe and healed)."

28

The Abrahamic Covenant is the Promise of Salvation

The Apostle Paul makes it clear that the Abrahamic covenant, is the promise of the "One" to come, the Messiah, the Savior of the world.

> *"¹⁵Brethren, I speak in the manner of men: Though it is only a man's covenant, yet if it is confirmed, no one annuls or adds to it.¹⁶Now to Abraham and his Seed were the promises made. He does not say, "And to seeds," as of many, but as of one, "And to your Seed," who is Christ. ¹⁷And this I say, that the law, which was four hundred and thirty years later, cannot annul the covenant that was confirmed before by God in Christ, that it should make the promise of no effect. ¹⁸For if the inheritance is of the law, it is no longer of promise; but God gave it to Abraham by promise"* **(Galatians 3:15-18).**

> *" .... in you shall **all the families of the earth shall be blessed***" **(Genesis 12:3).**

Jesus Inferred that the Abrahamic Covenant Confers Salvation

During His earthly ministry, Jesus said to Zacchaeus, the chief tax collector,

> *" .... Today **salvation has come to this house,** because he also is a son of Abraham;"* **(Luke 19:9).**

Jesus inferred that Zacchaeus, though unsaved at the time was in a position to receive salvation because, he was a descendant of Abraham. Everyone connected to Abraham has undeniable rights to the promise of salvation. The promise of salvation is through the 'One' to come; the 'Seed' of Abraham. Therefore, salvation is only found in that 'One' alone; the Savior, Jesus Christ. On this point the Apostle Peter remarked to the Jews of his days.

> *"Nor is there salvation in any other, for there is no other name under heaven given among men by which we must be saved"* **(Acts 4:12).**

If you are not saved, that is, you have not asked Jesus to be your Lord and Savior, you will have no right or access to these Covenant Blessings. But you can call upon Jesus now, ask Him to come into your heart and life. **Turn to page 123,** for a simple prayer you can say, **to receive Jesus. This will be the greatest decision you will ever make in your life. Congratulations!**

Faith in Christ connects you to the blessing of Abraham, and qualifies you for the benefits of salvation.

The Scriptures states:

> *"Therefore know that **only those who are of faith are sons of Abraham"** (Galatians 3:7).*

> **"If you belong to Christ, then you are Abraham's seed, and heirs according to the promise"** **(Galatians 3:29 NIV).**

Now that you have a good understanding of Redemption, Salvation and Covenant blessings, it will be much easier to grasp the truths in the next few chapters. Welcome to a journey of Unveiling the Implications of Redemption and Salvation. You will walk in victory and experience Abundant Living as you walk daily in these Covenant Realities.

---

[1] *International Standard Version (ISV) Copyright © 1995-2014 by ISV Foundation. ALL RIGHTS RESERVED INTERNATIONALLY. Used by permission of Davidson Press, LLC.*

[2] *Amplified Bible, Classic Edition (AMPC) Copyright © 1954, 1958, 1962, 1964, 1965, 1987 by The Lockman Foundation*

CHAPTER 1

ⓒⰔ℘Ⱄ

The Reality of Your Redemptive Provisions and Covenant Rights

---

"Therefore say to the children of Israel: 'I am the Lord; **I will bring you out** *from under the burdens of the Egyptians,* **I will rescue you** *from their bondage, and* **I will redeem you** *with an outstretched arm and with great judgments?"* **(Exodus 6:6).**

"In Him we have redemption through His blood, the forgiveness of sins, *according to the riches of His grace"* **(Ephesians 1:7).**

THE TRUTH THAT REDEMPTION (SALVATION) CONFERS ON YOU COVENANT RIGHTS

By Redemptive Provisions we mean, every benefit of salvation. Everything salvation has procured for the believer through the death and resurrection of Jesus, our Savior. Since salvation is a covenant promise, we call this covenant or redemptive provisions.

The benefits of salvation include eternal life (Revelation 5:9-10), Forgiveness of sins (Ephesians 1:7), Regeneration (2 Corinthians 5:17), Righteousness (Romans 5:17), Freedom from the Law's Curse (Galatians 3:13), Adoption into God's Family (Galatians 4:5), Healing (1 Peter 2:24), Deliverance from Sin's Bondage (Titus 2:14; 1 Peter 1:14-18), Peace with God (Colossians 1:18-20), Peace of God (Philippians 4:7), Spiritual Inheritance (1 Peter 1:4; Acts 26:18, Colossians 3:24) and the Indwelling of the Holy Spirit (1 Corinthians 6:19-20), just to mention a few.

To be saved then is to be forgiven: reborn, holy, justified, freed, adopted, healed, delivered from sin's hold, have peace, heir of God, reconciled and filled with the Holy Spirit.

Forgiveness of Sins Precedes Healing

"No one living in Zion will say, "I am ill"; and the sins of those who dwell there will be forgiven" **(Isaiah 33:24 NIV).**

"Then behold, they brought to Him a paralytic lying on a bed. When Jesus saw their faith, He said to the paralytic, "Son, be of good cheer; your sins are forgiven you" **(Matthew 9:2).**

Salvation Offers You Healing- Healing is A Redemptive Provision

*"So **ought not** this woman, being **a daughter of Abraham,** whom Satan has bound—think of it—for eighteen years, **be loosed from this bond** on the Sabbath?"* **(Luke 13:16).**

If you are saved, you are eligible for the benefits of Divine Health. Healing is your redemptive heritage and covenant right. If you are not saved, that is, you have not asked Jesus to be your Lord and Savior, you will have no right or access to these blessings.

A Word on Healing

If healing is a benefit of salvation, why do I still get sick? Well, it is a fact that covenant people still become sick, the woman in Luke 13:16, was sick (afflicted), though she was a daughter of Abraham. Many other saints were sick. We read the story of the two sisters (Mary and Martha), and their brother Lazarus, who were Jesus' friends. They confirmed that Jesus loved Lazarus.

If you are saved, you are eligible for the benefits of Divine health.

*"Therefore the sisters sent to Him, saying, **"Lord, behold, he whom You love is sick"** **(John 11:3).**

They said to Jesus, *'the one you love is sick'*, so it is possible that the ones Jesus loves can fall sick, but the good news is, that the believer can pray and receive healing because healing is promised to the redeemed; it is Redemptive Provision.

Covenant Promises for Divine Health

*"**If you** diligently heed the voice of the Lord your God and do what is right in His sight, give ear to His commandments and keep all His statutes, **I will put none of the diseases** on you which I have brought on the Egyptians. **For I am the Lord who heals you**",* **(Exodus 15:26).**

*"Behold, **I will bring it health and healing;** I will heal them and reveal to them the abundance of peace and truth"* **(Jeremiah 33:6).**

*"For **I will restore health to you and heal you of your wounds**, says the Lord ..."* **(Jeremiah 30:17).**

We understand that sin brought sickness into the world therefore, our world is sin-sick and plague with diseases. There are no promises that the Christian believer, once saved will not fall into sin anymore in this life, but there is promise of forgiveness just in case he falls into sin.

*"My little children, these things I write to you, **so that you may not sin. And if anyone sins**, we have an Advocate with the Father, Jesus Christ the Righteous"* **(1 John 2:1).**

Also, there are no promises that the believer will not fall sick in life, and just as we have promises in case we fall into sin, we have covenant promises in case we fall sick. The Bible says, *"who Himself bore our sins in His own body on the tree, that we, having died to sins, might live for righteousness—by whose stripes you were healed"* **(1 Peter 2:24).**

You are Rightly Positioned in the Covenant by Adoption

*" ⁴But when the fullness of the time had come, **God sent forth His Son,** born of a woman, born under the law,⁵to redeem those who were under the law, that we might receive the adoption as sons.⁶And because you are sons, God has sent forth the Spirit of His Son into your hearts, crying out, "Abba, Father!"⁷Therefore you are no longer a slave but a son, and if a son, **then an heir of God through Christ"*** **(Galatians 4:4-7).**

Notice, this verse says; Jesus came to redeem us, so that we might receive the adoption of sons, and all that pertain to Sonship. Sonship confers certain inalienable rights, we are now legal children, and as children we are God's heir, joint heir with Christ.

"And if children, then heirs—heirs of God and joint heirs with Christ, if indeed we suffer with Him, that we may also be glorified together" **(Romans 8:17).**

The Bible further states,

"... worthy is the Lamb who was slain to receive power and riches and wisdom, and strength and honor and glory and blessing!" **(Revelation 5:12).**

Christ the Lamb, is worthy to receive these Seven Fold Blessings, because He was slain (sacrificed), for us. The Worthy Lamb died to make us worthy. He received these blessings on our behalf, also as joint-heir with Him, every believer is entitled to these **Seven Fold Blessings**, (Power, Riches, Wisdom, Strength, Honor, Glory and Blessing).

Adoption gives You Rights to Family Inheritance

The Apostle Paul reaffirmed his life mission from the Lord Jesus, before King Agrippa while giving his testimony, he said **'the voice said to me'.**

"16But rise and stand on your feet; for I have appeared to you for this purpose, to make you a minister and a witness both of the things which you have seen and of the things which I will yet reveal to you. .... 17I now send you, 18to open their eyes, in order to turn them from darkness to light, and from the power of Satan to God, that they may receive forgiveness of sins and an inheritance among those who are sanctified by faith in Me" **(Acts 26:16-18).**

These words from the Lord Jesus reveals the pitiful state of the unregenerated soul (the unsaved) and the blessedness of the man who is saved by Christ. This verses also describes the mission of every God ordained minister and ministry. Notice Jesus said, after a man's eyes are opened, and he is turned from darkness to light, and from the power (or control) of Satan to God, he receives forgiveness of sins and **then inheritance** (redemption benefits) among those who are sanctified (Saints-the Family of God) in Him.

What is it Like to Be Outside the Family of God?

"That at that time you were without Christ, being aliens from the commonwealth of Israel, and strangers from the covenants of promise, having no hope, and without God in the world" **(Ephesians 2:12).**

Without Christ, means no salvation, *strangers from the covenants of promise;* means ineligible for the covenant-promises, *no hope in this world;* means hopeless, *without God in this world;* means Godless. What a horrid picture, a life without Christ. Life without Christ is life in deficit, but life with Christ is Life Abundant.

> Life without Christ is life in deficit, and life with Christ is Life Abundant.

The Mathematics of Redemption

Life – Christ (infinite worth) = (-Life in deficit).
Life + Christ (infinite worth) = (+Life Abundant).

CHAPTER 1

COVENANT REALITY

The Reality of Your Redemptive Provisions and Covenant Rights

THE TRUTH THAT REDEMPTION (SALVATION) CONFERS UPON YOU COVENANT RIGHTS

❖ To be saved then is to be forgiven; reborn, holy, justified, freed, adopted, healed, delivered from sin's hold, have peace, heir of God, reconciled and filled with the Holy Spirit.

❖ If you are saved, you are eligible for the benefits of Divine Health. Healing is your covenant heritage and redemptive right.

❖ You are rightly positioned in the covenant because of adoption.

❖ Adoption gives you rights to the family inheritance.

❖ Life without Christ is life in deficit, but life with Christ is Life Abundant.

Declarations:
"Let the Redeemed of the Lord say so, whom He has redeemed from the hand of the enemy" **(Psalm 107:2).**
"You will also decide and decree a thing, and it will be established for you ..." (Job 22:28 AMP).
I declare I am redeemed by the blood of Jesus therefore, free and delivered from every oppression of the enemy.

CHAPTER 2

The Reality of the Superiority of Your Covenant Status

"And he said to his people, "Look, **the people of the children of Israel are more and mightier than we"** (Exodus 1:9).

THE TRUTH ABOUT YOUR SPIRITUAL SUPERIORITY

Pharaoh's assessment of the Israelites was that they were *"more and mightier than them."* Now it was obvious that the Israelites were indeed numerous, but *mightier?* In reference to what? Nations today are rated as super-powers based on military might. Egypt at that time was a super power, but the Israelites were unorganized, unarmed, non-militant and simple people. So in what way, were they mightier or what could have elicited this comment from the king of Egypt? This has always been true of Israel, that their enemies have often realized that their strength is far beyond themselves.

*"For **their rock is not as our Rock, even our enemies themselves being judges"*** (Deuteronomy 32:31 KJV).

Pharaoh was neither delusional nor over exaggerating; the monarch made a statement which seemed to be a fact to him. There was something about the people that posed a threat to him. God said concerning Israel,

*" .... Your descendants will become well-known all over. Your children in foreign countries will be recognized at once **as the people I have blessed"*** (Isaiah 61:9 Message Bible).

The reality is that the enemy knows the truth about the strength of the church, more often than the church.

*"**He** increased His people greatly, and **made them stronger than their enemies"*** (Psalm 105:24).

41

*"And he said to his people, "Look, the people of the children of Israel are **more and mightier than we**"* **(Exodus 1:9).**

You Are More and Mightier

The believer is a 'New Creation' (2 Corinthians 5:17), 'A New Man', that is, he is born from above, therefore belong to a 'New Order'. The 'New Birth' confers on him a superior status in life. The scripture is filled with these assertions,'

The reality is that the enemy knows the truth about the strength of the church, more often than the church.

"For everyone born of God overcomes the world. This is the victory that has overcome the world, even our faith" **(1 John 5:4 NIV).**

*" …. We are **more than conquerors** …"* **(Romans 8:37).**

"…. ⁷There are more with us than are with him ⁸with him is an arm of flesh, but with us is the Lord our God" **(2 Chronicles 32:7-8).**

*"… If God is for us, **who can be against us?**"* **(Romans 8:31).**

When the Israeli spies came to Jericho, they visited Rahab's house and she confessed:

"⁹ᵃ And said to the men: "I know that the LORD has given you the land, that the terror of you has fallen

on us, and that all the inhabitants of the land are fainthearted because of you. [10]For we have heard how the LORD dried up the water of the Red Sea for you when you came out of Egypt, and what you did to the two kings of the Amorites who were on the other side of the Jordan, Sihon and Og, whom you utterly destroyed. "[11]And as soon as we heard these things, our hearts melted; neither did there remain any more courage in anyone because of you, for the LORD your God, He is God in heaven above and on earth beneath'" **(Joshua 2:9-11).**

"And Abimelech said to Isaac, **go away from us, for you are much mightier than we"** **(Genesis 26:16).**

The Believer is Superior to the Devil and His Cohorts

The enemy always has challenged the power and the authority of the Church, as he does also the believer, but Jesus promised victory over every opposition of the enemy. The believer or the church's power is not incontestable, but rather indomitable. Jesus said,

" .... I will build My church, and the gates of Hades shall not prevail against it" **(Matthew 16:18).**

Pharaoh's magicians and sorcerers, contested with Moses and Aaron, but in the end were publicly disgraced and defeated.

"¹⁰And Aaron cast down his rod before Pharaoh and before his servants, and it became a serpent. ¹¹But Pharaoh also called the wise men and the sorcerers; so the magicians of Egypt, they also did in like manner with their enchantments. ¹²For every man threw down his rod, and they became serpents. **But Aaron's rod swallowed up their rods**" (Exodus 7:10-12).

The Believer's Means of Warfare is Much More Superior

The believer's artillery is made by God, and he is dressed in the Armor of God, (Ephesians 6:11). Every piece of the armor is effectively designed by God with the enemy in mind, and also made to outlive the enemy's weapons.

"For the weapons of our warfare are not carnal but mighty in God for pulling down strongholds" **(2 Corinthians 10:4).**

Divine Assistance Makes God's People Mightier

The believer commands superiority in life because he is divinely assisted. Notice how the threat of the enemy against Israel by the Red Sea was completely squelched and how Pharaoh and his armies were forcefully and permanently silenced, because Israel had God's assistance.

The believer or the Church's power is not incontestable, but rather indomitable.

Divine Assistance Makes the Believer Victorious

*"And **He took off their chariot wheels**, so that they drove them with difficulty; and the Egyptians said, **"let us flee from the face of Israel, for the Lord fights for them** against the Egyptians"* **(Exodus 14:25).**

"³²It is God who arms me with strength, and makes my way perfect.³³He makes my feet like the feet of deer, and sets me on my high places"
(Psalm 18:32-33).

A SUPERIOR KINGDOM

The Kingdom of God is far superior to any known kingdom; the believer is a citizen of God's kingdom.

*"⁵...To him who loves us and has freed us from our sins by his blood, ⁶and **has made us to be a kingdom and priests to serve his God and Father**—to him be glory and power for ever and ever! Amen"*
(Revelation 1:5-6 NIV).

The Prophet Isaiah foretold the superiority of this kingdom as an endless one, an everlasting kingdom.

*"Of the increase of His government and peace **there shall be no end"* (Isaiah 9:7).**

Prophet Daniel also said,

"And in the days of these kings the God of heaven will set up a kingdom which shall never be destroyed; and

*the kingdom shall not be left to other people; it shall break in pieces and consume all these kingdoms, **and it shall stand forever**"* (**Daniel 2:44**).

John the Baptist announced the arrival of the Kingdom.

"In those days John the Baptist came preaching in the wilderness of Judea,[2]and saying, "Repent, for the kingdom of heaven is at hand!" (**Matthew 3:1-2**).

Far Above All

The scriptures assert that the risen Christ is seated at the right hand of God, and further says, that the Church (the body of Christ), is also raised up and seated together with Him in heavenly places, far above all other powers. The Church, (the body of Christ) is positionally placed far above any other powers, by virtue of the resurrection of Jesus Christ from the dead. The superiority and the far-above mentality of the believers, is not a pretentious attitude of arrogant, pious people, but is the in-Christ reality of the believer, and the language of the Scripture. The Bible says:

> *The superiority and the far-above mentality of the believers, is not a pretentious attitude of arrogant, pious people, but is the in-Christ reality of the believer, and the language of the Scripture.*

*"[20]which He worked in Christ when He raised Him from the dead and **seated Him at His right hand in the heavenly places,** [21]**far above all** principality and power and might and dominion, and every name that is named, not only in this age but also in that which is to*

come ... *⁶and raised us up together, and made us sit together in the heavenly places in Christ Jesus"* (Ephesians 1:20-21, 2:6).

DISPENSING KINGDOM BLESSINGS

Jesus commenced the Kingdom and commissioned His disciples, to go into the world to offer kingdom blessings to everyone they meet. The Church is established to service the needs of the world. Demons, diseases, and sickness are all a product of one kingdom, but freedom, health and healing are benefits of the Kingdom of Heaven.

"¹Then He called His twelve disciples together and gave them power and authority over all demons, and to cure diseases. ²He sent them to preach the kingdom of God and to heal the sick" (Luke 9:1-2).

"⁸Whatever city you enter, and they receive you, eat such things as are set before you. ⁹And heal the sick there, and say to them, 'The kingdom of God has come near to you'" (Luke 10:8-9).

The Kingdom Man or Woman

The Kingdom man or woman is a resourceful person in his or her sphere of influence. The believer is essential; he is needed, and he is relevant. He is salt (Matthew 5:13), therefore a change agent; he is to preserve and add flavor that is, meaning to people's lives. And like around many dinner tables, where people say, **"Please pass the salt"** the believer is in demand because of what he has to offer.

The Executors of Kingdom Affairs

The Church is God's instrument to showcase the power of the Kingdom; His purpose and His eternal plans in the world. The believer is therefore a trustee of the Kingdom of Heaven, an executor of Kingdom affairs. He is vested with Kingdom authority.

> *"And **I will give you the keys of the kingdom of heaven, and whatever you bind** on earth will be bound in heaven, **and whatever you loose on earth will be loosed in heaven"** (Matthew 16:19).*

> *"To the intent that now **the manifold wisdom of God might be made known by the church to the principalities and powers in the heavenly places"** (Ephesians 3:10).*

> *"⁶Let the high praises of God be in their mouth, and a two-edged sword in their hand; ⁷to **execute** vengeance on the nations, and punishments on the peoples; ⁸To bind their kings with chains, and their nobles with fetters of iron; ⁹to **execute** on them the written judgment— **This honor have all His saints.** Praise the Lord!" (Psalm 149:6-9).*

Thy Kingdom Come, Thy Will Be Done in Earth!

God wills that all men be saved (1 Timothy 2:3-4), thereby free from sin and the oppressions of Satan (Acts 26:16-18). He wills us to be in good health (1 John 3:2) and to contentedly enjoy all things that He has provided (1 Timothy 6:17). Therefore, the believer is to live out God's will on earth; he is to establish righteousness by Kingdom authority wherever he goes. The believer is to enforce the prayer, *"Thy Kingdom come, thy will be done, in earth ..."* (Matthew 6:10 KJV). The believer is to impose this prayer upon himself, his family, his church, his nation and on earth. Finally, he must adopt the far-above mentality, and be a practitioner of this

The Kingdom man or woman is a resourceful person in his or her sphere of influence. The believer is essential; he is needed, and he is relevant.

covenant reality. You are on your way to seeing mighty manifestations of God's power as His will is done in your life and around you. You are More and Mightier! And all the powers of darkness know that!

CHAPTER 2

COVENANT REALITY

The Reality of the Superiority of Your Covenant Status

THE TRUTH ABOUT YOUR SPIRITUAL SUPERIORITY

You are more and mightier.

* ❖ The believer or the church's power is not incontestable, but rather indomitable.

* ❖ The believer must adopt the far above mentality and must be a practitioner of this covenant reality.

* ❖ The Kingdom man or woman is a resourceful person in his or her sphere of influence. The believer is essential; he is needed, and he is relevant. He is salt (Matthew 5:13), therefore a change agent; he is to preserve and add flavor that is, meaning to people's lives.

* ❖ The believer is a trustee of the Kingdom of Heaven, an executor of Kingdom affairs. He is vested with Kingdom authority (Matthew 16:19).

* ❖ The believer is to establish God's will on earth, by the authority of the Kingdom wherever he goes. The believer is to enforce the prayer: *"Thy Kingdom come, thy will be done, on earth as it is in heaven"* (Matthew 6:10 KJV).

Declarations:
"Let the redeemed of the Lord say so..." (Psalm 107:2).
"You will also decide and decree a thing, and it will be established for you ..." (Job 22:28 AMP).

I declare, I am a kingdom man/woman, an ambassador of Christ, a trustee and an executor of Kingdom affairs. I am vested with kingdom authority. I am more than a conqueror, I am more and mightier, and greater is He that is in me, than he that is in the world. I am salt, and I am light in this world, I am relevant, and needed to add flavor to people's lives. I declare Lord, 'Thy kingdom come and Thy will be done on earth; thy will be done in my life, in my home, in my family, in my church, and in this nation, in Jesus Name, Amen!

CHAPTER 3

❧

The Reality of
Your
Spiritual Potential

---

*" .... let us deal shrewdly with them,
lest they multiply, ..."*
(Exodus 1:10).

THE TRUTH ABOUT THE UNLIMITED INFLUENCE OF YOU REACHING YOUR SPIRITUAL CAPACITY

Pharaoh's concern was about Israel's future; that is, Israel's potential or what Israel could be. Potential is the capacity to develop into something in the future. People around us respond either positively by encouraging us to cultivate our potential or negatively by discouraging us from developing and reaching our potential.

" .... *let us deal shrewdly with them, lest they multiply* ..." **(Exodus 1:10).**

What would happen if the Israelites grow to be more than they were already? They were already *more and mightier.* Pharaoh did not want them to grow any further. If they grew to a certain number, they might be able to defend themselves. There was a time the Philistines kept Israel defenseless by making sure that they had no blacksmiths to make

> *Spiritual immaturity will leave you defenseless, and a cheap victim of Satan and his cohorts.*

weapons to defend themselves. Imagine, there were no weapons for the army. Spiritual immaturity will leave you defenseless, and a cheap victim of Satan and his cohorts.

"[19]There were no blacksmiths in the land of Israel in those days. The Philistines wouldn't allow them for fear they would make swords and spears for the Hebrews, **[22]So on the day of the battle none of the people of Israel had a sword or spear ...**"
(1 Samuel 13:19, 22 NLT).

Pharaoh anticipated the potential power of Israel's continuous growth, and therefore planned to stop them from further growth. The effectiveness of military strategy depends entirely upon whether all possibilities have been foreseen. A military war strategist once said that, *"anticipation is key to winning any war"*. Anticipation produces readiness, readiness leads to preparation, and preparation is key in winning any war.

What is Spiritual Potential?

God has already deposited all the resources and the gifts you need to fulfill your destiny, that is, His purpose and plan for your life. These gifts need to be discovered, developed, and then deployed. Anointings, giftings, ministries or life assignments come in stages or levels. As you put forth efforts to grow; you will begin to tap into and draw from your *Your personal gift is to lead you to develop into a full stature in Christ, where you can operate in your full capacity.* divine reserves to release your full potential. Your personal gift is to lead you to develop into a full stature in Christ, where you can operate in your full capacity.

There is Always a Force Against Anything or Anyone Rising

It takes more power for the airplane to take off, than it takes for it to cruise in the air. There is always a force against anything or anyone rising. The enemy will resist you growing into your full potential in Christ. In commercial greenhouse and nursery production, croppers use chemicals as one of many ways to control crop height. Crops can grow very tall and become unmanageable in greenhouses and nurseries, and so to eliminate this problem, croppers use chemical retardants. In this way they can achieve crop-specific height, by applying the right plant growth retardants

Check for growth retardants in your spiritual life, whatever might be hindering your growing into your rightful place in the body of Christ.

(PGRs). Check for growth retardants in your spiritual life, whatever might be hindering your growing into your rightful place in the body of Christ. The enemy is concerned that you might grow more in influence or develop more of your spiritual faculties. What would happen in the world, if the body of Christ discovers, develops and deploys the unlimited power of the Holy Spirit in the world?

The Devil Fears You Might Grow to Realize Your Full Potential in Christ

One of the greatest concerns of the Devil, is your spiritual growth. He fears you might grow to realize your full potential in Christ. What would happen if you grow more in spiritual power and increase in spiritual knowledge, wisdom, and spiritual

Imagine the difference in your life and the powerful impact in the life of others around you, from growing more in prayer and making much of the grace of God.

understanding? Imagine the difference in your life and the powerful impact in the life of others around you, from growing more in prayer and making much of the grace of God upon your life.

The Grace Capacity

The Apostle Paul challenged the Corinthian Christians on this subject of ensuring that they do not receive God's grace in vain, but fully utilizing the grace capacity on their lives.

> *"We then, as workers together with Him also plead with you **not to receive the grace of God in vain**"* **(2 Corinthians 6:1).**

> *"But by the grace of God I am what I am: and his grace which was bestowed upon me was not in vain; but I labored more abundantly than they all: yet not I, but the grace of God which was with me"* **(1 Corinthians 15:10 KJV).**

The Apostle Paul shared his secret of growing in Christ, with the Philippian Church:

> *"**Not that I have already attained**, or am already perfected; **but I press on**, that I may lay hold of that for which Christ Jesus has also laid hold of me"* **(Philippians 3:12).**

In other words, I am constantly striving so that, I may be able to reach my spiritual capacity; thereby releasing my full potential, and fulfilling the purpose for which Christ (the Messiah) called me.

Problem with Spiritual Immaturity

As long as the heir is underage, that is immature, he is at the mercy of his caretakers (the house servants) who determine what and when he will eat, what he will wear, and when he will play or sleep. He is not able to enjoy the full benefit of his status as heir until he comes of age, that is, the age he is officially recognize as an adult. He will continue to be commanded, instead of being in command.

*"¹What I am saying is that **as long as an heir is underage, he is no different from a slave,** although he owns the whole estate.²The heir is subject to guardians and trustees until the time set by his father.³So also, when we were underage, we were in slavery under the elemental spiritual forces of the world.⁴But when the set time had fully come, God sent his Son, born of a woman, born under the law,⁵to redeem those under the law, that we might receive adoption to Sonship"* **(Galatians 4:1-5 NIV).**

We read that until Israel became strong, (that is, grew strong), they were not able to subdue their enemies. The secret of living in dominion is in spiritual maturity. If you are not growing, you will be groaning.

"And it came to pass, when Israel was strong, that they put the Canaanites under tribute ..." **(Judges 1:28).**

The Power that Works Within the Believer is Limitless

The Holy Spirit is the power that works in the believer and this power is limitless. What the Holy Spirit can achieve in and through the believer in the world is immeasurable. If you yield yourself to Him, He is able to release the spiritual capacity in you, taking you from grace to grace and from glory to glory.

> *"Now unto Him that is able to do exceeding abundantly above all that we ask or think, **according to the power that works in us**"* **(Ephesians 3:20).**

> *"But you shall receive power when the Holy Spirit has come upon you ..."* **(Acts 1:8).**

Anointing is in Measures

Anointing is for a purpose, therefore the anointing upon a person is indicative of their particular assignment. Also, anointing is in measures or is quantifiable; this is why Elisha, the apprentice-prophet asked for a double portion of his master's anointing (2 Kings 2:9). If there a double portion, then there is a portion, and so on. It was only said of Jesus, that He was given the Spirit without measure, that is, limitless (John 3:34).

Releasing Spiritual Potential by Changing Levels

David

David was first introduced as a shepherd boy, in the field; then we see him in the king's court, a skilled musician; from there a Captain in the king's army and then a king in Israel; and finally, as a prophet of God. It was the same man, but he functioned in different levels of anointing (assignments). David grew from one level into another, thereby releasing his potential and fulfilling his God-ordained purpose. Your life's assignment is like your big shoes or clothes; and like the old folks will say *"you will grow into it."* The process is that of growing into each assignment or next level God calls you into.

> *"⁵Whatever Saul asked David to do, David did it successfully. So Saul made him a commander over the men of war, an appointment that was welcomed by the people and Saul's officers alike. ¹⁴David continued to succeed in everything he did, for the Lord was with him.... ¹⁶But all Israel and Judah loved David because he was so successful at leading his troops into battle"* **(1 Samuel 18:5, 14, 16 NLT).**

Releasing Your Potential Step by Step

As a little shepherd boy David had certain character qualities that God was looking for in appointing a king. He was dependable and showed genuine care for the flock and his father's business. He displayed rare courage, as he faced off with a lion and a bear. The point is that, whatever he had, wherever he was, he perfected his skills and qualified himself for the next place God wanted to take him. The Law of Progression and Divine Promotion demands satisfactory discharge of responsibilities on the present level, before advancement to the next level. God teaches us in steps. David noted this in one of his Psalms:

> *The point is that, whatever he had, wherever he was, he perfected his skills and qualified himself for the next place God wanted to take him.*

*"**The steps** of a good man are ordered by the Lord, And He delights in his way"* **(Psalm 37:23).**

Notice he said 'the steps', and not the strides. If you were to come down from a stage, you will do well if you take the steps. You might hurt yourself if you avoid the steps and insist on taking a stride downstage. Many do not want to take necessary steps or go through the process, they will like to arrive at destiny in an instant, be a pastor in one week, or a prophet overnight.

The Sling, the Staff, and the Stones

Many are not winning in life because they are not able to transfer what they have learned on the ground onto the battleground. As a shepherd, David learned the tools of the shepherd (the sling, the staff and

> *Many are not winning in life because they are not able to transfer what they have learned on the ground onto the battleground.*

learned how to throw stones). And when the day came to fight Goliath, he used what he had, that is, what he was used to. What he learned on the field he brought to the battlefield. This is called transferred or applied skill. The purpose of classroom learning is to be able to transfer the knowledge to everyday living.

"So he shepherded them according to the integrity of his heart, and guided them by the skillfulness of his hands" **(Psalm 78:72).**

The Strings and the Songs

David was King Saul's private musician. He was highly recommended by a palace official who knew his father Jesse.

"One of the young men spoke up, "I know someone. I've seen him myself: the son of Jesse of Bethlehem, an excellent musician. He's also courageous, of age, well-spoken, and good-looking. And God is with him" **(1 Samuel 16:18 MSG).**

As a musician he earned the National Title, "The sweet Psalmist of Israel";

"Thus says David the son of Jesse; Thus says the man raised up on high, the anointed of the God of Jacob, And the sweet psalmist of Israel: ²" The Spirit of the Lord spoke by me, And His word was on my tongue" **(2 Samuel 23:1-2).**

His music was exemplary; anointed and exalting. David's songs are timeless, elating and very comforting. He was able to soothe a demon oppressed king, by his anointed music.

The Sword and the Shield

As Captain of the Israeli Army, David was a skillful fighter with great martial abilities. He was a competent swordsman, led many raids and was able to subdue the enemies of Israel. When Absalom, David's son rebelled against him Hushai the king's counsellor, said this to the young man, about David:

> *"You know your father and his men; they are fighters,* and as fierce as a wild bear robbed of her cubs. *Besides, your father is an experienced fighter;* he will not spend the night with the troops"
> **(2 Samuel 17:8 NIV).**

The Scepter

David was most distinguished above all the kings of Israel because of his personal devotion to God. He was a God-lover; therefore, his major impact was religious. He reformed worship in the land; writing and arranging worship songs, and installed priests, and musicians who were available in shifts for temple worship. As king in Israel he ruled with the Scepter of Righteousness and Justice, thereby brought peace and prosperity to the land.

> *"By the blessing of the upright **the city is exalted** ..."*
> **(Proverbs 11:11a).**

The Seer (Prophet)

David was an uncommon man, in the sense that his devotion to God never waned neither did he lose his passion for God, even as king. Most studies on David omit this point that he wasn't just king in Israel, but he died as a prophet of God. As a prophet, he gave the Old Testament saints a prototype of the Messiah (The Prophet-King), and a glimpse into the New Covenant Blessings, through his songs. Psalms 22 and 110 are just a couple of his prophetic (Messianic) songs.

"The Spirit of the Lord spoke by me, And His word was on my tongue" **(2 Samuel 23:2).**

David rose to greatness by faithfully perfecting his gifts on every level. From the primitive tools of a shepherd boy, to the more sophisticated tools of a soldier, he was a master at every level. Ever wonder, if the delay in realizing your dreams is caused by your failing to master the level you are on. Maybe all you have right now is a primitive tool; an ordinary rod like Moses, a humble ministry. The fruit is from the tree, but the tree is from the seed; though the seed looks very small and insignificant, destiny lies hidden in that small thing in your hand. Well, why don't you try and make the best of what you have and where you are, and you

Ever wonder, if the delay in realizing your dreams is caused by your failing to master the level you are on

The fruit is from the tree, but the tree is from the seed, though the seed looks very small and insignificant, destiny lies hidden in that small thing in your hand.

will be surprised, how it will grow and reveal the greatness hidden on the inside of you.

Esther

The young Jewish maiden slave in Persia, who one day became Queen over all the land. From being her uncle's favorite, to the king's favorite.

Joseph

A young slave in Potiphar's house, with notable leadership qualities. It was said of Joseph, that he became very successful. "A successful slave", hard to imagine, right? Where masters are failing, slaves are succeeding. Notice that everywhere he was, his leadership quality was always bringing him to the forefront, until finally he became Second in Command (Prime Minister), of the foremost nation in his time, from the manager of Potiphar's house to the manager of the whole country.

Faithfulness on one level qualifies you for the next level. It is through this process you both release and realize your spiritual capacity. Notice all these people kept growing and operating in different levels of their assignments, thereby releasing, realizing and reaching their full potential. On the other hand, we see Samson, who was destined to deliver Israel from the Philistines as foretold before his birth, but unfortunately did not fulfil his God ordained purpose, nor realized His full potential in God.

> *Faithfulness on one level qualifies you for the next level. It is through this process you both release and realize your spiritual capacity.*

"Lest they multiply (grow more)" (Exodus 1:10).

The Admonition to Grow

"But grow in the grace and knowledge of our Lord and Savior Jesus Christ. To Him be the glory both now and forever. Amen" **(2 Peter 3:18).**

*[5]"But also for this very reason, giving all diligence, **add to your faith** virtue, to virtue knowledge,[6]to knowledge self-control, to self-control perseverance, to perseverance godliness,[7]to godliness brotherly kindness, and to brotherly kindness love.[8] For if these things are yours and abound, you will be neither barren nor unfruitful in the knowledge of our Lord Jesus Christ.[9]For he who lacks these things is shortsighted, even to blindness, and has forgotten that he was cleansed from his old sins.[10]**Therefore, brethren, be even more diligent to make your call and election sure, for if you do these things you will never stumble;** [11]for so an entrance will be supplied to you abundantly into the everlasting kingdom of our Lord and Savior Jesus Christ"* **(2 Peter 1:5-11).**

The Measure of the Stature of the Fullness of Christ

*"**Till we all come** in the unity of the faith, and of the knowledge of the Son of God, **to a perfect man, to the measure of the stature of the fullness of Christ"*** **(Ephesians 4:13).**

To develop to the full stature in Christ, is the believer's life's goal. The believer has to continually strive to grow and increase in every area of life. There are many advantages to spiritual growth. The benefit of spiritual growth is that; it enhances the development of other areas of the personality. It positively promotes the physical, emotional, mental-intellectual and social aspects of life as well, and development in these areas brings personal power. Spiritual growth is key to victorious living. Spiritual growth will lead to spiritual power, and once you are empowered, you will cease to be dominated by your circumstances, influenced by the world, and harassed by the Devil.

> *The benefit of spiritual growth is that; it enhances the development of other areas of the personality. It positively promotes the physical, emotional, mental-intellectual and social aspects of life as well, and development in these areas brings personal power.*

CHAPTER 3

COVENANT REALITY

The Reality of Your Spiritual Potential

THE TRUTH ABOUT THE UNLIMITED INFLUENCE OF YOU REACHING YOUR SPIRITUAL CAPACITY

The Devil fears you might grow to realize your full potential in Christ.

- ❖ Spiritual immaturity will leave you defenseless and a cheap victim of Satan and his cohorts.

- ❖ As you put forth efforts to grow; you will begin to tap into and draw from your divine reserves, to release your full potential.

- ❖ Your personal gift is to lead you to develop into a full stature in Christ, where you can operate in your full capacity.

- ❖ What would happen if you grow more in spiritual power; and increase in spiritual knowledge, wisdom, and spiritual understanding?

- ❖ Imagine the difference in your life and the powerful impact in the life of others around you, from growing more in prayer and making much of the grace of God.

❖ Faithfulness on one level qualifies you for the next level. It is through this process we both release and realize our spiritual capacity.

❖ The Law of Progression and Divine Promotion demands satisfactory discharge of responsibilities on the present level, before advancement to the next level. God teaches us in steps.

❖ Many are not winning in life because they are not able to transfer what they have learned on the ground onto the battleground.

❖ The benefit of spiritual growth is that it enhances the development of the other areas of the personality. it positively promotes the physical, emotional, mental-intellectual and social aspects of life as well, and development in these areas brings personal power.

❖ Spiritual growth is key to victorious living. Spiritual growth will lead to spiritual power, and once you are empowered, you will cease to be dominated by your circumstances, influenced by the world, and harassed by the Devil.

Declarations:
"Let the redeemed of the Lord say so..." (Psalm 107:2).
"You will also decide and decree a thing, and it will be established for you ..." (Job 22:28 AMP).

I declare victory over spiritual stagnation, victory over every spiritual growth retardant in my life. I shall make spiritual progress from now on in Jesus Name.

CHAPTER 4

⚮

The Reality of the Source of All Spiritual Warfare and Afflictions

---

"Therefore they did set over them taskmasters to afflict them with their burdens. And they built for Pharaoh Treasure cities, Pithom and Raamses" **(Exodus 1:11 KJV).**

THE TRUTH THAT AFFLICTION IS A TOOL OF THE ENEMY TO KEEP YOU DOWN

The Hebrew word used here is 'annotow', it means to afflict, to violate, or to be bowed down, and only occurs twice in the Old Testament (Exodus 1:11, 2 Samuel 13:22).

Why Was Israel Afflicted?

The enemy's reaction to Israel's prosperity was to introduce affliction in order to affect their further increase (posterity). But God allowed the enemy's plan knowing that this will serve to prepare and toughened them, for the arduous wilderness journey that lay ahead of them. It seemed that the work that grace began with prosperity in Goshen, must be perfected with austerity for the wilderness journey.

Satanic Afflictions as Means to Hinder Abundant Life

There are different ways in which afflictions comes to the believer. Satan instigates most of the afflictions, but other afflictions come as a direct result of personal neglect of moral duty or instructions, in this case, Satan takes advantage of the opportunity to cause afflictions.

The Method of Afflictions

All the names given to Satan in the Bible describes the several forms in which he has acted, to carry out his villainous tasks. Satan has many ways in which he carries out his activities in the world, his methods are innumerable; he seems to have a scheme for every theme. He works through afflictions; deceptions, hindrances, murders,

Satan tries to afflict the whole man, he attacks the body, the mind and the soul, in order to hinder the believer's spiritual progress and assignments.

slanders, fears, enchantments, spells, curses, divinations, evil covenants, paralyzing the prayers of many saints. I shall only discuss in this chapter satanic afflictions, that is, afflictions originated by Satan.

Satan tries to afflict the whole man, he attacks the body, the mind and the soul, in order to hinder the believer's spiritual progress and assignments. Whenever affliction is prolonged, Satan tries to make us think and feel that God has abandoned us, and cause us to doubt the truth we have believed.

Satan Can Induce All Forms of Afflictions

Physical Afflictions: Physical Deformities (Luke 13:11-17), Disabilities, Blindness (Matthew 12:22), and Dumbness (Matthew 9:32-33).
Mental and Emotional Afflictions: Mental Illness, Insanity (Matthew 8:28-34), Psychological Problems.
Spiritual Afflictions: (Job 1:12, 2 Corinthians 12:7).

God Permits Some Afflictions

God does permits some afflictions whenever it can be useful for the development of the believer's character and also to unfold His plan, as in the case of Job. It is comforting to know that all the afflictions that God permits, He sees to it that they turn out to be purposeful and rewarding in the end. See the next chapter for the benefits of trials. If God permits it, then it has a purpose and it will run its course, we cannot stop, rebuke or pray this away. We can

It is comforting to know that all the afflictions that God permits, He sees to it that they turn out to be purposeful and rewarding in the end.

only ask and appropriate the grace given to us during the trial.

Paul

The Apostle Paul wrote about a messenger of Satan that was sent to buffet him. With God's permission Satan took occasion to afflict Paul, but God had a purpose to allow the affliction (the messenger of Satan), to keep Paul from the sin of pride, that is being exalted above measure. At least, this is how the Apostle understood it.

> *"And lest I should be exalted above measure by the abundance of the revelations, a thorn in the flesh was given to me, a messenger of Satan to buffet me, lest I be exalted above measure"* (**2 Corinthians 12:7**).

Whatever this messenger of Satan represents we are not told, but it is clear that it created a painful experience in three dimensions.

Physical Pain- It was a physical condition, (a thorn in the flesh).

Psychological and Mental Pain- It was prolonged and agonizing.

Spiritual Pain- A messenger of Satan, and unanswered prayer.

Jesus' Ministry to the Afflicted

> *"How God anointed Jesus of Nazareth with the Holy Spirit and with power, who went about doing good and* **healing all who were oppressed by the devil,** *for God was with Him"* (**Acts 10:38**).

*"So **ought not this woman, being a daughter of Abraham,** whom Satan has bound—think of it—for eighteen years, **be loosed from this bond** on the Sabbath?"* **(Luke 13:16).**

Throughout the gospel we see Jesus healing those oppressed or afflicted by the devil. Sickness is an oppression of the Devil. This woman we are told by Luke, the Physician-Gospel writer, had a *'spirit of infirmity'*. Luke was a physician, but he pointed out that this woman's case was non clinical, but rather spiritual. Jesus said, this was the work of the Devil. The Devil kept this woman down for eighteen years.

It is clear from this story that affliction is a tool of Satan to hinder people, especially the believer from his assignments and from fulfilling God's purpose in life. Sickness is the work of the evil one who comes *"to steal, to kill and to destroy"* (John 10:10).

God Wants You Well

"Beloved, I wish above all things that thou mayest prosper and be in health, even as thy soul prospereth" **(3 John 2 KJV).**

When Peter's mother in-law was healed (Luke 4:39), she got up and served Jesus and those who were in her house. Unless you are free you cannot serve God fully. You need to be freed from satanic bondages, and also from personal bondages, i.e., ambitions, worldly pursuits, alliances and allegiances, until then you cannot serve God wholly.

- God is aware of all your afflictions.
- All afflictions are conceived and designed by the Devil.
- All afflictions from the devil are intended for evil.
- God does not permit all afflictions.
- God permits some afflictions.
- All afflictions permitted by God turns out to be helpful in the end.
- No afflictions can come to the believer unless permitted by God.

CHAPTER 4

COVENANT REALITY

The Reality of the Source of All
Spiritual Warfare and Afflictions

THE TRUTH THAT AFFLICTION IS A TOOL OF THE ENEMY TO KEEP YOU DOWN

You can overcome the worst of all Satanic Trials.

- ❖ Satan tries to afflict the whole man, he attacks the body, the mind and the soul, in order to hinder the believer's spiritual progress and assignments.

- ❖ God does permits some afflictions, whenever it can be useful for the development of the believer's character and also to unfold his plan, as in the case of Job.

- ❖ Affliction is a tool of Satan to hinder people, especially the believer from his assignments and from fulfilling God's purpose in life.

- ❖ God wants you well.

- ❖ You need to be freed from satanic bondages, and also from personal bondages, i.e., ambitions, worldly pursuits, alliances and allegiances, until then you cannot serve God fully.

Declarations:
"Let the redeemed of the Lord say so..." (Psalm 107:2).
"You will also decide and decree a thing, and it will be established for you ...." (Job 22:28 AMP).

I declare freedom from personal bondages, evil alliances, and ungodly allegiances. I declare freedom from every oppression of the Devil. I declare no weapon of affliction, or infirmity, or evil counsel, fashioned against me shall prosper, in Jesus Name, Amen!

CHAPTER 5

❧

The Reality
of the
Benefits of Trials

---

*"But the more they afflicted them,
the more they multiplied and grew ..."*
(Exodus 1:12).

THE TRUTH THAT GOD USES THE SAME AFFLICTION TO BUILD YOU UP

Anyone sailing the seas understands this one indisputable fact, that there is no way to stop the ocean waves, control the strong winds, or the occasional unsuspecting storms. These are the constants on the seas. So it is, sailing through life. The believer is constantly assailed by many troubles; however, the child of God has a promise of victory over all his challenges. The Psalmist said,

> *"Many are the afflictions of the righteous, but the Lord delivers him out, of them all"* **(Psalm 34:19).**

The enemy brings afflictions and plans evil against the believer, but God uses the same affliction to build up and advance the believer's life's purpose.

Running with Patience

> *"Wherefore seeing we also are compassed about with so great a cloud of witnesses, let us lay aside every weight, and the sin which doth so easily beset us, and **let us run with patience** the race that is set before us"* **(Hebrews 12:1 KJV).**

The Christian life is compared to a race, and in order to finish the course or fulfill destiny, we are admonished to get rid of everything that will hinder our race, and to run with patience (perseverance-endurance). Endurance is key to winning marathon races. Life is filled with many challenges: surprises, detours, delays and dead-ends, it is impossible to overcome all of life's huddles without patiently enduring.

Patience is an admirable virtue (character), patience is a perfecter; it is the quality-character that helps to finish whatever one began. It is the strength of persistence, and it is only produced by the testings, and the trying of faith.

"*Knowing that* **the testing of your faith produces patience**" **(James 1:3).**

The Trying of Faith is for the Development of Character

The trying of faith produces character. The trying of your faith brings out the best in you. Character is the most important asset of any man alive; it is the only thing he takes to heaven. God is more interested in your character than your comfort. There are graces and virtues the Holy Spirit has deposited in you, these need to be developed in order for you to become Christ-like and enjoy the Abundant Life. God therefore takes you through different stations and stages of development to be able to release these in you. Everything you will ever need is in you.

The Beating, the Bruising, the Crushing, and the Squeezing is to Release the Hidden Resources

Notice that most precious things in life are hidden, because the habit of nature is to hide its treasures. And it takes real hard work and determination to unearth these treasures. The oil is in the depth of the earth, the diamond is found in the dirt, the pearls in the oyster's shell,

The habit of nature is to hide its treasures.

is way down deep in the ocean, the refreshing coconut juice is hidden within layers and inside a hard shell.

The iron is beaten, the grapes are crushed, the orange is squeezed and the wheat is threshed to give their resources. And whenever a rose petal is bruised, it releases its fragrant oil. It is through the beating, the bruising, the crushing, and the squeezing that we get the treasures hidden inside these elements; likewise, it is through the testings and the trials that character is produced in us.

> *"These trials will show that your faith is genuine. It is being tested as fire tests and purifies gold--though your faith is far more precious than mere gold. So when your faith remains strong through many trials, it will bring you much praise and glory and honor on the day when Jesus Christ is revealed to the whole world"* **(1 Peter 1:7 NLT).**

The words testing and trying in these two verses (James1:3, 1 Peter 1:7), are used to describe the process of refining gold. The aim of refining gold is to rid it of its impurities. As Job also said,

> *"But He knows the way that I take; when He has tested me, I shall come forth as gold"* **(Job 23:10).**

What is the Outcome of Persecution or Affliction?

> *"But the more they afflicted them, **the more they multiplied and grew ....**"* **(Exodus 1:12).**

Notice that the afflictions brought about by Pharaoh did not hinder the children of Israel, but rather advanced their purpose. The Egyptians had tried everything to suppress the children of Israel, they had made their lives bitter in hard bondage, but instead of the Israelites becoming downcast and their population diminishing, they continued to grow more than ever. *"The more they afflicted them, the more they grew".*

The word translated *'grew'*, is the Hebrew word, *'Parat'*, which is related to another Hebrew word *'Perez'*, (Genesis 38:29), which means, "to break forth", "burst through" and or "spread everywhere." In order words, the more they oppressed them, the more they spread everywhere as water after breaking through a dam. History has shown that persecutions against the Church, only have advanced her cause and in unusual ways have strengthened the believers. Jesus said,

> *"... I will build my church, and all the powers of hell will not conquer it"* **(Matthew 16:18 NLT).**

The Trying of Faith is Purposeful and Towards a Profitable End

*"²My brethren, count it all joy when you fall into various trials, ³knowing that **the testing of your faith produces patience. ⁴But let patience have its perfect work, that you may be perfect and complete, lacking nothing'.** ... .. ¹²Blessed is the man who endures temptation; for **when he has been approved, he will receive the crown of life** which the Lord has promised to those who love Him"* **(James 1:2-4,12).**

Joseph

Long before the Exodus, Joseph explained to his brothers that God had turned around their evil plans for his good.

> *"But as for you, **you meant evil against me; but God meant it for good,** in order to bring it about as it is this day, to save many people alive"* **(Genesis 50:20).**

David

David also wrote of the benefits of trials.

> *"**Before I was afflicted I went astray**, but now I keep Your word"* **(Psalm 119:67).**

> *"**It is good for me that I have been afflicted, that I may learn** Your statutes"* **(Psalm 119:71).**

Paul the Apostle

> *"… The things which happened to me have actually turned out for **the furtherance of the gospel**"* **(Philippians 1:12).**

Also to the Church in Corinth he wrote,

> *"No temptation has overtaken you except such as is common to man; but God is faithful, who will not allow you to be tempted beyond what you are able, but with the temptation will also make the way of escape, that you may be able to bear it"* **(1 Corinthians 10:13).**

The Church in Corinth had their share of problems and were also familiar with the Apostle Paul's personal trials. He wrote to them as a fellow sufferer, with the aim to strengthening them in their season of trials. He wanted them to know;

First of all, that righteous suffering (the believer's testings') should be viewed from heaven's perspective, because it's only then, does afflictions become meaningful and profitable. Notice that in the Kingdom, afflictions are translated into *'weights of glory'*.

> *"For our light affliction, which is but for a moment, is working for us a far more exceeding and eternal weight of glory"* **(2 Corinthians 4:17).**

Secondly, suffering is temporary (transitory).
"Troubles don't always last, this too shall pass".

Finally, suffering is a beneficial device working for our good.
We owe more to our troubles and difficulties than we do acknowledge, they have been our greatest instructors. The truth is we learn only little from our blessings. Moses said to Israel that God led them

> *We owe more to our troubles and difficulties than we do acknowledge, they have been our greatest instructors.*

through the wilderness, to train and prepare them for where He was taking them.

*"... To humble and test you **so that in the end it might go well with you"** (Deuteronomy 8:16 NIV).*

The Apostle confidently says *'suffering is achieving for us'* and other translations of the same verse repeat the same idea,' *producing for us'* or *'working out for us.'*

*"For our present troubles are small and won't last very long. **Yet they produce for us** a glory that vastly outweighs them and will last forever!"*
(2 Corinthians 4:17 NLT).

*"For this our light and transitory burden of suffering is **achieving for us** .... a weight of glory"*
(2 Corinthians 4:17 Weymouth).

Also in another place Apostle Paul writes,

*"And we know that **all things work together for good** to those who love God, to those who are the called according to His purpose"* **(Romans 8:28).**

The Double Reality

Note these five scripture verses; whenever you read the word **suffering,** it is also followed by the word **glory**, as contradicting as these two terms may be, it is very comforting to know, that the believer's sufferings are not without gain.

*"... if indeed **we suffer with Him,** that we may also be **glorified together"** (Romans 8:17).*

*"For I consider that **the sufferings** of this present time are not worthy to be compared with **the glory** that is to be revealed to us"* **(Romans 8:18).**

*"But rejoice, inasmuch as ye are partakers of **Christ's sufferings**; that, when **his glory** shall be revealed, ye may be glad also with exceeding joy"* **(1 Peter 4:13 KJV).**

*"The elders who are among you I exhort, I who am a fellow elder and a witness of **the sufferings** of Christ, and also a partaker of **the glory** that will be revealed"* **(1 Peter 5:1).**

*"For this our light and transitory burden of **suffering** is achieving for us .... a weight of **glory**"* **(2 Corinthians 4:17 Weymouth).**

The Lord will not forsake the righteous and will not permit any trial in his life, which He has not first of all supervised, (1 Corinthians 10:13). The believer's tests are purposeful and are a part of God's master plan for his life. The believer has the promise of victory in every battle and God

Your challenges do not change your Covenant status or your in-Christ realities.

brings all of the believer's trials and testing to a meaningful and useful end. Your challenges do not change your covenant status or your 'in-Christ' realities.

85

Consider This Wonderful Revelation

"No temptation has seized you except what is common to man. And God is faithful; he will not let you be tempted beyond what you can bear. But when you are tempted, he will also provide a way out so that you can stand up under it" **(1 Corinthians 10:13 Berean Study Bible).**

1. **Your trials are not uncommon:** *"No temptation has seized you except what is common to man".* Your trials are not rare, or unusual. Somebody had gone through the same thing you are going through now, and somebody else will yet go through the same thing after you. There is nothing new under the sun.

2. **God can be trusted during your difficult trials:** *"God is faithful."* You can count on His unfailing love, to sustain you through your times of difficulty. *"Yet have I not seen the righteous forsaken"* **(Psalm 37:25).**

3. **God supervises every trial:** *"He will not let you be tempted beyond what you can bear."* Notice the phrase **"He will not"**, suggest that God is still in control. He permits or disallows trials that are unbearable for you. Therefore, God has to know what the trial is, in order to determine whether or not, you are able to bear it. He supervises every one of your trials.

4. **Every trial brings a blessing:** *"But when you are tempted, He will also provide a way out."* The KJV translation says, *"but with the temptation will also make*

the way of escape." Notice the words **'also'** and **'with'**, in both translations. This suggests that the trials cannot come alone, or without a way of escape (relief). No trouble ever knocks on your door without a blessing. Therefore, look for the way of escape instead of feeling closed in. Look for the sweet fruit from the bitter tree of troubles. Every trial offers therefore, a life lesson.

5.   **Trials ordained by God will not destroy you:** *"so that you can stand up under it."* The trial that God allows to come to the believer is never intended for his ruin. God sees to it that you survive it, "stand up under it." The trials will come and go, but true faith in Christ will

> *No trouble ever knocks on your door without a blessing. Therefore, look for the way of escape instead of feeling closed in.*

outlast the storms and at last, the believer will still be standing. This is the truth of the irrepressible nature of a Christ-like faith.

CHAPTER 5

COVENANT REALITY

The Reality of the Benefits of Trials

THE TRUTH THAT GOD USES THE SAME AFFLICTION TO BUILD YOU UP

You will be better by it.

* Endurance is key to winning marathon races. Life is filled with many challenges, surprises, detours, delays and dead-ends it's impossible to overcome all of life's huddles without patiently enduring.

* Notice that the precious things of life are hidden, because the habit of nature is to hide its treasures. And it takes real hard work and determination to unearth these treasures.

* The iron is beaten, the grape is crushed, the orange is squeezed and the wheat is threshed to give their resources. And whenever a rose petal is bruised, it releases its fragrant oil. It is through the beating, the bruising, the crushing, and the squeezing that we get the treasures hidden inside these elements, likewise it is through the testings and the trials that character is produced in us.

* The believer's tests are purposeful and are a part of His master plan for his life.

❖ Your challenges do not change your covenant status or your "In-Christ" realities.

❖ No trouble ever knocks on your door without a blessing. Therefore, look for the way of escape instead of feeling closed in.

Declarations:
"Let the redeemed of the Lord say so..." **(Psalm 107:2).**
"You will also decide and decree a thing, and it will be established for you ...." (Job 22:28 AMP).

I declare none of my trials shall turn me into a bitter man/woman, but shall make me a better man/woman in Jesus Name. I receive grace to endure trials, courage to be patient and faith to overcome every trial in Jesus Name, Amen!

CHAPTER 6

❀

The Reality of the Remarkable Impact of A Christ-like Life

" .... The Egyptians dreaded and were
exasperated by the Israelites"
(Exodus 1:12 AMP).

THE TRUTH THAT A DEVOTED CHRISTIAN IS GRIVEOUS TO THE DEVIL

"But the more they afflicted them, the more they multiplied and grew. ***And they were grieved because of the children of Israel"*** *(Exodus 1:12 KJV).*

Grieved! How is it, that the oppressor is grieved by the oppressed? The Egyptian's oppression and cruel treatment of Israel, had not produced expected results, instead the people were getting stronger. The more they oppress them, the more they became unmanageable until their oppressors were exasperated! The truth is, whenever God's people are in compliance with His Word and in His favor they are indomitable.

The truth is, whenever God's people are in compliance with His Word and in His favor; or in compliance with His word and His will, they are indomitable.

The Fear of Israel is Upon Other Nations

"This day I will begin to put ***the dread and fear of you upon the nations*** *under the whole heaven, who shall hear the report of you, and shall tremble and be in anguish because of you"* **(Deuteronomy 2:25).**

"No man shall be able to stand against you; ***the Lord your God will put the dread of you and the fear of you upon all*** *the land where you tread, just as He has said to you"* **(Deuteronomy 11:25).**

*"And they journeyed, and **the terror of God was upon the cities** that were all around them, and they did not pursue the sons of Jacob"* **(Genesis 35:5).**

Could you cause grief to the Devil? Yes! A Christ-like faith is irrepressible, and an irrepressible faith is grievous to the Devil.

The Irrepressible Nature of a Christ-like Faith

The Scriptures features men and women, who made remarkable impact in the world through their irrepressible faith. No matter what challenges they faced, or battles they had to fight, they held out until they won the victory, and left behind a legacy of winning faith. They served God by accomplishing great exploits in their generations; they took back surrendered grounds, built up the old ruins, took territories, pushed the enemy back, defended their inheritance, raised the standards, and established God's will on earth, these men and women were grievous and did terrified the Devil.

A Christ-like faith is irrepressible, and an irrepressible faith is grievous to the Devil.

The Remarkable Influence of a Devoted Life

The Agenda of the *'god of this world'* is to suppress righteousness and the righteous ones; but a righteous man in position of authority can have great influence over his community and the world. When righteousness is established the Devil is grieved.

"By the blessing [of the influence] of the upright the city is exalted, but by the mouth of the wicked it is torn down" **(Proverbs 11:11 AMP).**

Joseph

Joseph was a God-fearing man, whose commitment to right living led him to a most notable position in Egypt. And by his godly leadership he was able to save his family; the nation of Egypt and the other nations of his time. The devoted Christian is a resourceful person in his or her sphere of influence and a hamper to the work of the enemy.

"Then Pharaoh said to his officials, 'Isn't this the man we need? Are we going to find anyone else who has God's spirit in him like this?'" **(Genesis 41:38 MSG).**

Joshua

Joshua was also a devoted man whose great influence, was a terror to the enemies of God. We read of his great exploits, how he secured the Promised Land for Israel. He dispossessed the people who occupied the land and delivered it to Israel as God promised them. He killed every king and every entity standing in the way of possessing their possessions. His name and his fame was so terrifying to other nations, that the Gibeonites, came in pretense as friends in order to be spared by him (Joshua 9).

"16Thus Joshua took all this land: the mountain country, all the South, all the land of Goshen, the lowland, and the Jordan plain—the mountains of Israel and its lowlands, 17.... He captured all their kings, and struck them down and killed them. 18Joshua made war a long time with all those kings.19There was not a city that

made peace with the children of Israel, except the Hivites, the inhabitants of Gibeon. All the others they took in battle" **(Joshua 11:16-19).**

Caleb

At 80 years old, most people would have given up on their dreams, but Caleb was ready to go out to war in order to realize his dreams; to possess his possessions and take delivery of his promised destiny. What a challenge from an eighty-year old man!

*"As yet I am as strong this day as on the day that Moses sent me; **just as my strength was then, so now is my strength for war,** both for going out and for coming in"* **(Joshua 14:11)**.

Elijah

The solitary Prophet of God who defeated four hundred Baal prophets on Mount Carmel, and turned Israel back to God. Oh! That we have men like Elijah again, to stand against idolatry in our nation and boldly declare the Word of the Lord. One Christ-like life will change the world. When the king of Israel saw Elijah, he called him the nation's trouble maker.

*"… When Ahab saw Elijah, that Ahab said to him, **"Is that you, O troubler of Israel?"*** (**1 Kings 18:17**).

David

David was a remarkable Biblical character, he was referred to as the man after God's heart, because of his devotion to God. As king of Israel, and a worshipper of God, he brought national reform in worship and discouraged idolatry. In fact, he made it his duty to stamp out the wicked and the idolaters.

> *"My daily task will be to ferret out the wicked and free the city of the LORD from their grip"* **(Psalm 101:8 NLT)**.

David's righteous influence also grew beyond Israel, as he was respected and feared in other surrounding nations.

> *"16So David did as God commanded him, and they drove back the army of the Philistines from Gibeon as far as Gezer.17Then the fame of David went out into all lands, and the Lord brought the fear of him upon all nations"* **(1 Chronicles 14:16-17)**.

Daniel

As a young man Daniel lived in Babylon; but refuse to be defiled by the world around him. His commitment to live holy, made him to become God's mouthpiece to kings and their empires. He overcame the seduction of Babylon, and leave us a legacy of how to live godly in an ungodly world. Daniel was singled out as having superior wisdom and understanding. All the king's wise men could not match his insight. And when they conspired against him and threw him in the lion's den, even the lions would not touch him. A righteous man is a problem for the Devil and his cohorts. True faith in God outlast the storms.

> *"There is a man in your kingdom, in whom is the Spirit of the Holy God. And in the days of your father, light and understanding and wisdom, like the wisdom of the gods, were found in him ...."* **(Daniel 5:11)**.

The Christ Life

From the beginning to the end of His life, Jesus' ministry was an interference against the works of the Devil. The Bible states:

" .... *For this purpose,* **the Son of God was manifested, that He might destroy the works of the devil**" **(1 John 3:8b).**

"how God anointed Jesus of Nazareth with the Holy Spirit and with power, who went about doing good **and healing all who were oppressed by the devil,** *for God was with Him"* **(Acts 10:38).**

When a demon-possessed man saw Jesus, the demons cried out and asked Jesus why He was interfering with their evil work. The demons acknowledged Him as the Son of the Most High God; they knew who He was. It is interesting to note that there is no question as to Jesus' identity in the spiritual realm, it is only among men that His identity is a subject of debate. The Devil is not worried about you, if you are not interfering with him. You are not a threat to the Devil until your life is a disruption to his kingdom and business.

The Devil is not worried about you, if you are not interfering with him. You are not a threat to the Devil until your life is a disruption to his kingdom and business.

"With a shriek, he screamed, **"Why are you interfering with me, Jesus, Son of the Most High God?** *In the name of God, I beg you, don't torture me!"* **(Mark 5:7 NLT).**

*"Then the Pharisees [argued and] said to one another, 'You see that your efforts are futile. **Look! The whole world has gone [running] after Him!'"** (John 12:19 AMP).*

Paul

The Apostle Paul was once under the control of religious spirits; he was self-righteous and fanatically misguided (zealous), he was persecuting the church of Christ (Galatians 3:5-6). He was so deceived as to believe he was serving God. However, when he met Jesus (Acts 9:5), and came into the knowledge of truth and grew in grace and power, he became a nuisance to the Devil.

"And the evil spirit answered and said, 'Jesus I know, and Paul I know; but who are you?'" **(Acts 19:15).**

Paul and Silas

Paul and Silas were beaten mercilessly and imprisoned in Philippi, for preaching and delivering a slave girl with the spirit of divination who made much profit for her masters. Fortune telling and psychic readings are huge business in big cities, but the preaching of the Gospel and the liberation of people can be loss of profit for some business sector. The girl's masters said of Paul and Silas:

*" .... These men, being Jews, **exceedingly trouble our city"** (Acts 16:20).*

And as soon as they were released from prison they went on to Thessalonica, where they started a revival which led to a riot by the Jews, who opposed them. The Jews said,

" .... These who have turned the world upside down, have come here too" **(Acts 17:6).**

It is interesting that this statement was made about only two people, these two people have turned the world upside down. No matter the opposition Paul and Silas faced, they were unstoppable neither did they cease from their work. When you also mature in grace and in the knowledge of God, your life will begin to interfere with the Devil. The truth is that a mature disciple is a force in the world.

Peter and John

As we attempt to live Biblical Christianity, the Holy Spirit will produce Pentecost results through us that will puzzle the people around us. We will impact our communities and change the world around us. Peter and John had healed a man born lame (Acts 3:1-10), and this gave them the opportunity to preach the Good News about Jesus. This miracle caused a stir in the city and many of the people came to faith in Jesus. If the temple and the worshippers represents the old order of religion, then Peter and John represents a new order -the Church- and the lame man represents lame humanity. The answer for lame humanity is the Church, the Church is the only hope for humanity.

> *As we attempt to live Biblical Christianity, the Holy Spirit will produce Pentecost results through us that will puzzle the people around us.*

The church has the power to put men and women back on their feet. Therefore, a cold, powerless Christian cannot represent Christ duly in the world. Peter and John were arrested, jailed and now on trial for preaching in Jesus' Name.

> *"What are we going to do with these men?"* they
> asked. *"Everyone living in Jerusalem knows they have
> performed a notable sign, and we cannot deny it"*
> **(Acts 4:16 NIV).**

These officials were not lacking ideas as to how to deal
with accused men or offenders, but the question at hand was
asked as a result of the difficulty between what these men
were accused of and the
remarkable, visible
miracle done by them
and witnessed by
everyone in the city. For
the people in the city
knew that the man now
standing on his two feet was born lame.

*Let it be known that the Church
will not be able to represent
Christ duly in this world if she
remains cold, unconcern,
powerless and lethargic.*

Many of us have not been in a position where people
around us ask this kind of puzzling question, our faith has not
yet produced this kind of unquestionable results.

Today's Christianity has put many on Easy Street;
where their Biblical knowledge is preserved, their peace,
undisturbed, their courage unchallenged, their spiritual gifts
unstirred, their faith noncontagious and their alabaster boxes
yet unbroken therefore, the oil is not flowing. Yet we wonder
why the world around us is unchanging. Could it be that the
world is not seeing the evidence of Pentecost as in the case of
these early disciples. Let it be known that the Church will not
be able to represent Christ duly in this world if she remains
cold, unconcern, powerless and lethargic.

The World Need to See the Evidence of Pentecost

*"For the earnest expectation of **the creation eagerly waits for the revealing of the sons of God"*** **(Romans 8:19).**

The world is waiting for the revealing of the sons of God. The 'Sons' are the matured children; those who have come of age. They know who they are, they understand their assignments and know what hour it is now. They have their lamps trimmed and burning, they are busy but waiting and watching, for the Bridegroom's return.

The world is surprisingly tired of the ordinary, they themselves believe there must be more than these. They have heard our songs, listened to our messages, eaten our church dinners and the Saturday morning breakfasts, they have visited the thrift shops and benefited from the soup kitchens, but now, they need something more than the handouts.

The world is surprisingly tired of the ordinary, they themselves believe there must be more than these.

They need supernatural encounters with the Holy Ghost that will leave them breathless in the presence of God. They need the manifestation of God's power that will save their restless souls, shake their world, arrest their vain minds, and leave them in awe of the unquestionable power of Pentecost. It is time the Church wakes up from deep slumber, and traces her steps back to the upper room for a new drenching of power, for rain, the latter rain and for a new day of Pentecost.

The Prophet Isaiah said to the children of Israel:

100

"Awake, awake! Put on your strength, O Zion; Put on your beautiful garments, ... ²*Shake yourself from the dust, arise; Sit down, O Jerusalem! Loose yourself from the bonds of your neck, O captive daughter of Zion!"* **(Isaiah 52:1-2).**

Notice that the message was directed to God's people. The children of Israel had to fight the spirit of slumber then, the Church also has to fight the same spirit now. The spirit of dullness, the spirit responsible for apathy. The prophet's admonition is now also upon us; the Church must come awake, rise up and take her stance again because we are now in the last hour.

*"*¹¹*And do this, knowing the time, that now it is high time to awake out of sleep; for now, our salvation is nearer than when we first believed.* ¹²*The night is far spent; the day is at hand. Therefore, let us cast off the works of darkness, and let us put on the armor of light"* **(Romans 13:11-12).**

Pray Against the Spirit of Slumber

Many people love their sleep and wish not to wake up or be disturbed, but it is dangerous to be asleep at the wrong time. Jesus said to Peter, James and John 'watch and pray, so that you will not fall into temptation' (Mark 14:38 NIV), but instead of watching and being alert they were overwhelmed with sleep. They slept then, but cried later. Pray that the Spirit of the Lord will start a fire in your soul, keep it burning so you will be awake when the Lord comes. The devil is not worried about sleeping saints, he is only afraid of saints 'Alive'.

CHAPTER 6

COVENANT REALITY

The Reality of the Remarkable Impact of
A Christ-like Life.

THE TRUTH THAT A DEVOTED CHRISTIAN
IS GRIVEOUS TO THE DEVIL

You are causing him (the Devil) grief.

- ❖ A Christ-like faith is irrepressible, and an irrepressible faith is grievous to the Devil.

- ❖ When righteousness is established the Devil is grieved.

- ❖ *Joseph*: The devoted Christian is a resourceful person in his or her sphere of influence and a hamper to the work of the enemy.

- ❖ *Daniel:* A righteous man is a problem for the Devil and his cohorts.

- ❖ *Elijah*: One Christ-like life will change the world.

- ❖ *Paul & Silas*: The truth is that a mature disciple is a force in the world.

❖ The Devil is not worried about you, if you are not interfering with him. You are not a threat to the Devil until your life is a disruption to his kingdom and plans.

❖ As we attempt to live Biblical Christianity, the Holy Spirit will produce Pentecost results through us that will puzzle the people around us.

❖ Peter and John represents a new order -the Church- and the lame man represents lame humanity. The answer for lame humanity is the Church, the Church is the only hope for humanity. The church has the power to put men and women back on their feet

❖ Let it be known that the Church will not be able to represent Christ duly in this world, if she remains cold, unconcern, powerless and lethargic.

❖ The world is surprisingly tired of the ordinary, they themselves believe there must be more than these.

Declarations:
"Let the redeemed of the Lord say so..." **(Psalm 107:2).**
"You will also decide and decree a thing, and it will be established for you ...." (Job 22:28 AMP).

I declare, I am the salt of the earth, I am a change agent, I am relevant, essential, and I am needed. I shall not lose my effectiveness in Jesus Name.

CHAPTER 7

The Reality of
Divine Favor
on Your Life

---

*"¹⁹And the midwives said to Pharaoh,
because **the Hebrew women are not as
the Egyptian women;** for they are lively,
and are delivered ere the midwives come in to them.
²⁰Therefore God dealt well with the midwives:
and the people multiplied, and waxed very mighty"*
(Exodus 1:19-20 KJV).

THE TRUTH THAT GOD DOES FAVOR HIS PEOPLE

"Surely, LORD, you bless the righteous; **you surround them with your favor as with a shield"** (Psalm 5:12 NIV).

The Hebrew women were not like the Egyptian women, because of Divine Favor. The word translated *lively* here means vigorous. A striking fact is that this was said about a race of people, "the Hebrew women," not just one or few, but all of them. God favored them with vitality. God is able to "give life to our mortal bodies" (Romans 8:11). It was said of Moses, *"Moses was 120 years old when he died, yet his eyesight was clear, and he was as strong as ever"* (Deuteronomy 34:7 NLT).

Caleb also testified to a special kind of undiminishing vitality at the age of 80 years.

"I am still as strong today as the day Moses sent me out; *I'm just as vigorous to go out to battle now as I was then"* **(Joshua 14:11 NIV).**

The Multi-Sided Favor of God

Protecting Favor

Abraham, Isaac and Jacob all enjoyed the protecting favor of God, in many ways. God gave Abraham an unusual victory, when he went against a Four-king Alliance Army, with just 318 servants to rescue his nephew Lot (Genesis 14:16). Also, in Genesis 12:13, we read

God is able to engineer circumstances to your favor.

how Abraham in order to save his life endangered Sarah's life. Pharaoh would have taken Sarah for his wife, except that God intervened. God showed favor to Abraham, even though he acted in a selfish manner. This was an unmerited favor. God is able to engineer circumstances to your favor.

Protecting Favor: The Three Hebrew Boys

Shadrach, Meshach and Abednego were officials of the King of Babylon; they were in charge of the provinces of Babylon. As officers they were responsible to enforce the king's orders in their different spheres of influence, but a day came when these men disobeyed the king's orders themselves. They refused to bow down to the king's idol, since this was contrary to their faith and a breach of their devotion to Jehovah. They did not care that they would lose their good jobs, the special comforts and their royal privileges as king's officials; it was more important to them to stay true to God. As a result, they had to face the consequence of defying the king which meant death, in a burning fiery furnace.

Even though, Shadrach, Meshach and Abednego, lost favor of their earthly master, they were still in favor with the God of heaven.

Even though Shadrach, Meshach and Abednego lost favor of their earthly master, they were still in favor with the God of heaven. God's favor never leaves the righteous in times of trouble. In the furnace of affliction, these men experienced God's protecting favor. Divine favor shielded them from the fiery furnace.

"Surely, LORD, you bless the righteous; **you surround them with your favor as with a shield"** (Psalm 5:12 NIV).

Protecting Favor: David

Protecting favor is the miracle of protection that makes it impossible for your enemy to fulu7fil his desires upon your life. King Saul was bent on killing David; he hired assassins after David, and several times he personally went out on a manhunt for David. As a result, David spent many months out in the wilderness hiding from king Saul.

"And David stayed in strongholds in the wilderness, and remained in the mountains in the Wilderness of Ziph. **Saul sought him every day,** *but God did not deliver him into his hand"* **(1 Samuel 23:14).**

On one occasion David had gone to hide in the wilderness of Ziph. The Ziphites were descendants of Judah, that makes them David's countrymen and naturally he would have supposed he would find protection and support there among his own people, especially since he was an innocent man. But, unfortunately the Ziphites turned on David and twice they betrayed him, by telling King Saul about his hideouts. Instead of them being David's confidants they offered themselves as King Saul's allies.

"²⁵When Saul and his men went to seek him, they told David. Therefore, he went down to the rock, and stayed in the Wilderness of Maon. And when Saul heard that, he pursued David in the Wilderness of Maon.²⁶ Then Saul went on one side of the mountain, and David and his men on the other side of the

*mountain. **So David made haste to get away from Saul, for Saul and his men were encircling David and his men to take them**"* **(1 Samuel 23:25-26).**

King Saul and his men came down to capture David, and it was not looking good for David. Notice the story says that David was trapped by Saul's troops. What do you do when you are surrounded by enemies and closed in on every side? Any ideas on how to escape blood thirsty, ruthless, violent men? David had nowhere to turn, except to turn to God. He cried out to God in this moment of desperation and God intervened for him, because God's favor was upon his life. David said,

> *"¹⁰For my enemies speak against me; And those who lie in wait for my life take counsel together, ¹¹Saying,'God has forsaken him; Pursue and take him, for there is none to deliver him.' ¹²O God, do not be far from me; **O my God, make haste to help me!**"* **(Psalm 71:10-12).**

Notice how God protected David and saved him just in time from his enemies. I pray you will receive a timely help from God today, Amen!

The Miracle of Intervention

> *"²⁷But a messenger came to Saul, saying, **'Hurry and come, for the Philistines have invaded the land!' ²⁸ Therefore Saul returned from pursuing David**, and went against the Philistines; **so they called that place the Rock of Escape**"* **(1 Samuel 23:27-28).**

As far as King Saul was concerned David was nothing but a dead dog, trapped with no way of escape. Just then, the king got urgent news -bad news- that the Philistines, the old enemy of Israel were invading the land. The king had to choose between chasing one man to satisfy his desire or go back to fight the Philistines to save the nation and secure his throne. He decided to go and fight the Philistines and was forced to call off the attack on David. David knew it was the Lord that rescued him that day. David wrote Psalm 54 during this time of difficulty.

David was a man of varied experiences; he leaves us with examples on how to deal with our problems and lessons on what to do in moments of despair. In another Psalm, David reflects:

"¹The Lord is my light and my salvation; Whom shall I fear? The Lord is the strength of my life; Of whom shall I be afraid? ² When the wicked came against me to eat up my flesh, my enemies and foes, they stumbled and fell. ³ Though an army may encamp against me, my heart shall not fear; Though war may rise against me, in this I will be confident. ⁴ One thing I have desired of the Lord, that will I seek: That I may dwell in the house of the Lord all the days of my life, to behold the beauty of the Lord, and to inquire in His temple. ⁵ *"For in the time of trouble He shall hide me in His pavilion; In the secret place of His Tabernacle He shall hide me; He shall set me high upon a rock. ⁶ And now my head shall be lifted up above my enemies all around me;* Therefore, I will offer sacrifices of joy in His tabernacle;

I will sing, yes, I will sing praises to the Lord" **(Psalm 27:1-6)**.

These are not just words of a man who was a poet but the reflections of a man who had experienced God's protecting favor. This Psalm was birth out of deep reflections and recollections of his times of troubles and the protecting favor of God. If a man can remember his helplessness, he can also appreciate the depth of mercy he received from God. Reflections and thanksgiving are fuel for the traveler's soul.

> *If a man can remember his helplessness, he can also appreciate the depth of mercy he received from God.*

You know what will happen if you don't stop to refuel because you are too busy driving. Stop! And give thanks. If you can think you will thank.

Providential Favor

"And God is able to make all grace abound toward you, that you, always having all sufficiency in all things, may have an abundance for every good work" **(2 Corinthians 9:8)**.

Isaac experienced providential favor during a time of famine. He sowed in faith and in obedience to God's instruction and received a hundred-fold harvest in the time of famine. This was clearly Divine Favor, unheard-of-favor.

*" 12Then **Isaac sowed in that land, and reaped** in the same year **a hundredfold; and the Lord blessed him**.13The man began to prosper, and continued prospering until he became very prosperous;14for he had*

*possessions of flocks and possessions of herds and a great number of servants. So **the Philistines envied him"*** **(Genesis 26:12-14).**

The Nation of Israel

Israel experienced a forty-year, daily provision during their wilderness journey.

*"And **the children of Israel ate manna forty years,** until they came to an inhabited land; **they ate manna until they came to the border of the land of Canaan"*** **(Exodus 16:35).**

Distinguishing Favor

This is the kind of favor that sets an individual apart. Joseph, Namaan, Esther, David, and Daniel, all received this kind of favor. They were highly favored and blessed.

Joseph was Distinguished as a Slave in His Master's House

This kind of favor is unquestionable to unbelievers. Joseph's master could see that the Lord was with Joseph, and credited his success to Divine favor. I pray for this kind of distinguishing favor over your life.

*"²The Lord was with Joseph, and he was a successful man; and he was in the house of his master the Egyptian. ³And his master saw that the Lord was with him and that **the Lord made all he did to prosper in his hand"*** **(Genesis 39:2-3).**

David was Distinguished Above
All the Kings of the Earth

*"²⁰I have found My servant David; with My holy oil I have anointed him,²¹With whom My hand shall be established; also My arm shall strengthen him.²²The enemy shall not outwit him, nor the son of wickedness afflict him.²³I will beat down his foes before his face, and plague those who hate him.²⁴But My faithfulness and My mercy shall be with him, and in My name his horn shall be exalted.²⁵Also I will set his hand over the sea, and his right hand over the rivers.²⁶He shall cry to Me, 'you are my Father, My God, and the rock of my salvation.'²⁷Also **I will make him my firstborn, the highest of the kings of the earth.**²⁸My mercy I will keep for him forever, and My covenant shall stand firm with him.²⁹His seed also I will make to endure forever, and his throne as the days of heaven"* **(Psalm 89:20-29).**

Solomon was Distinguished Above
All the Kings of Israel and All the Nations

*"²⁹And **God gave Solomon wisdom and exceedingly great understanding, and largeness of heart like the sand on the seashore.** ³⁰**Thus Solomon's wisdom excelled the wisdom of all the men of the East and all the wisdom of Egypt.** ³¹**For he was wiser than all men** —than Ethan the Ezrahite, and Heman, Chalcol, and Darda, the sons of Mahol; and his fame was in all the surrounding nations.³²He spoke three thousand proverbs, and his songs were one thousand and five.³³Also he spoke of trees, from the*

cedar tree of Lebanon even to the hyssop that springs out
of the wall; he spoke also of animals, of birds, of creeping
things, and of fish.[34]**And men of all nations, from all
the kings of the earth who had heard of his
wisdom, came to hear the Wisdom of Solomon"(1
Kings 4:29-34).**

Daniel

We read of young Daniel in Babylon:

*"Now **God had brought Daniel into favor and
tender love with the prince of the eunuchs"* (Daniel
1:9).**

Job

Job was distinguished by favor above all the men in the
East.

*"... So that **this man was the greatest of all the
people of the East"* (Job 1:3)**

The Nation of Israel is Distinguished by Favor

*"For **You are the glory of their strength; and in your
favor our horn is exalted"** (Psalm 89:17).*

*"I will make a difference between my people and your
people ... "* **(Exodus 8:23).**

*"[4]And the Lord will make a difference between the
livestock of Israel and the livestock of Egypt. So nothing
shall die of all that belong to the children of Israel, ...'
[6]So the Lord did this thing on the next day, and all the*

livestock of Egypt died, but of the livestock of the children of Israel, not one died" **(Exodus 9:4,6).**

"Has any god ever tried to take for himself one nation out of another nation, by testings, by signs and wonders, by war, by a mighty hand and an outstretched arm, or by great and awesome deeds, like all the things the LORD your God did for you in Egypt before your very eyes?" **(Deuteronomy 4:34 NIV).**

*"And **who is like your people Israel--the one nation on earth that God went out to redeem as a people for himself,** and to make a name for himself, and to perform great and awesome wonders by driving out nations and their gods from before your people, whom you redeemed from Egypt?"* **(2 Samuel 7:23 NIV).**

*"He caused **all who held them captive to show them mercy***" **(Psalm 106:46 NIV)**

"But the LORD will have mercy on the descendants of Jacob. He will choose Israel as His special people once again. He will bring them back to settle once again in their own land. And people from many different nations will come and join them there and unite with the people of Israel" **(Isaiah 14:1 NLT).**

"Blessed are you, Israel! Who is like you, a people saved by the LORD? He is your shield and helper and your glorious sword. Your enemies will cower before you, and you will tread on their heights" **(Deuteronomy 33:29 NIV).**

*"Now if you obey me fully and keep my covenant, **then out of all nations you will be my treasured possession. Although the whole earth is mine"** (Exodus 19:5 NIV).*

Exceptional Favor

This kind of favor happens when God overrules the rules to bless you. It may be getting a loan you were not qualified for, getting admission into a place above your head, or getting a job without the necessary qualifications. This favor singles you out, it will even fetch you out from obscurity. When this favor is at work, 'Your case is different'. You become an exception to the rules. I pray you receive this kind of favor today in Jesus Name, Amen!

The Widow of Zarephath
The widow of Zarephath, received a special visitation from God that saved her family from death by starvation. Jesus said that there were many needy widows in Israel in the days of Elijah, during the three-and-a-half-year famine, but Elijah was not sent to any of them *except* to the Widow of Zarephath.

*"25But I tell you truly, many widows were in Israel in the days of Elijah, when the heaven was shut up three years and six months, and there was a great famine throughout all the land, 26but to none of them was Elijah sent **except to Zarephath,** in the region of Sidon, **to a woman who was a widow"** (Luke 4:25-26).*

Namaan

This Captain of the Syrian Army received a special favor from God as there were many lepers in Syria when he was healed.

"And many lepers were in Israel in the time of Elisha the prophet, and none of them was cleansed **except Namaan** *the Syrian"* **(Luke 4:27).**

Mary the Mother of Jesus

The angel told Mary that she was blessed and highly favored among women.

"And having come in, the angel said to her, 'Rejoice, **highly favored one,** *the Lord is with you;* **blessed are you among women!'"** **(Luke 1:28).**

I pray that you will be the object of this kind of favor from God today, in Jesus Name.

Favor in Answer to Prayers

God favors the prayers of His people. He said,

*"**If my people,** which are called by my name, shall humble themselves, and pray, and seek my face, and turn from their wicked ways;* **then will I hear from heaven, and will forgive their sin, and will heal their land"** **(2 Chronicles 7:14).**

*"**You will also decide and decree a thing, and it will be established for you;** And the light [of **God's***

favor] will shine upon your ways" (Job 22:28 AMP).

"And it shall come to pass, that before they call, I will answer; and while they are yet speaking, I will hear" (Isaiah 65:24 KJV).

"¹²On the day the Lord gave the Israelites victory over the Amorites, Joshua prayed to the Lord in front of all the people of Israel. He said, "Let the sun stand still over Gibeon, and the moon over the valley of Aijalon'.¹³So the sun stood still and the moon stayed in place until the nation of Israel had defeated its enemies. Is this event not recorded in The Book of Jashar? The sun stayed in the middle of the sky, and it did not set as on a normal day.¹⁴There has never been a day like this one before or since, when the Lord answered such a prayer. Surely the Lord fought for Israel that day!" (Joshua 10:12-14 NLT).

Uncommon Favor

Esther

Esther was distinguished among the maidens in Persia. Esther is a picture of the reality of God's favor. We read that, she obtained **'favor'** of the custodian, then she obtained '**favor of all'** the people, and finally, she obtained '**more than all favor'** from the king who made her his queen.

"⁹Now the young woman pleased him, and she obtained his favor; so he readily gave beauty preparations to her, besides her allowance. Then seven choice maidservants

were provided for her from the king's palace, and he moved her and her maidservants to the best place in the house of the women, ... '15And **Esther obtained favor in the sight of all** *who saw her'* ... 17**The king loved Esther more than all** *the other women, and* **she obtained grace and favor in his sight more than all** *the virgins; so he set the royal crown upon her head and made her queen instead of Vashti"* **(Esther 2:9, 15, 17).**

Only God's favor can put a crown on the head of an orphan, and turn a slave girl into a queen. When God's favor is at work, you might not need a resume or experience to get the job. Joseph did not need a resume or experience to become Egypt's Prime Minister. One minute of God's favor is better than one hundred years of labor. Pray for this kind of favor over your life.

Great Favor

You do not need to pray for great favor, you already have great favor. You received great favor the moment you were saved by Jesus, Alleluia! Salvation is the greatest mercy (grace or favor) we have received from God.

*"4**But God, who is rich in mercy,** because of **His great love with which He loved us,** 5even when we were dead in trespasses, made us alive together with Christ** (by grace you have been saved),* 6 **and raised us up together, and made us sit together in the heavenly places in Christ Jesus"** (Ephesians 2:4-6).

"From his abundance we have all received one gracious blessing after another" **(John 1:16 NLT).**

Hadad

"And **Hadad found great favor in the sight of Pharaoh,** *so that he gave him as wife the sister of his own wife, that is, the sister of Queen Tahpenes"*
(1 Kings 11:19).

Favored for Life

"For His anger is but for a moment, **His favor is for a lifetime ....** *'"* **(Psalm 30:5 AMP).**

God's favor is for life, it's new every morning and last our lifetime. If His favor is for a lifetime, it stands to reason therefore, that we have His favor every day and also can ask for special favors every day. How should we live LIFE then? This way, *Living In His Favor Everyday'*, (L.I.F.E.). The Lord promised never to stop doing good *(favoring)* for His people.

"22 .... His compassions fail not.23They are new every morning ..." **(Lamentations 3:22-23).**

"And I will make an everlasting covenant with them: ... **I will never stop doing good for them"** **(Jeremiah 32:40 NLT).**

The Hebrew Midwives Were Favored by God
for Their Reverence for God

The Hebrew midwives did not fear Pharaoh above God, even though they knew that their disobedience of the king's order could lead to their deaths, but they were strong in the face of this hard trial. As Prophet Daniel said, *"…. those who know their God shall be strong"* (Daniel 11:32b).

> *"The fear of man brings a snare: but whoever puts his trust in the LORD shall be safe"* **(Proverbs 29:25).**

The Fear of the Lord Brings Favor

> *"Blessed* **and favored by God is the man who fears** *[sin and its consequence] at all times …"* **(Proverbs 28:14 AMP).**

> *"When a man's ways please the Lord, He makes even his enemies to be at peace with him"* **(Proverbs 16:7).**

> *"¹Blessed* **is everyone who fears the Lord,** *who walks in His ways.²When* **you eat the labor of your hands, you shall be happy, and it shall be well with you.** *³Your wife shall be like a fruitful vine in the very heart of your house, Your children like olive plants all around your table. ⁴Behold, thus shall the man be blessed who fears the Lord.⁵The Lord bless you out of Zion, and may* **you see** *the* **good** *of Jerusalem* **all the days of your life.**⁶*Yes, may* **you see your children's children.** *Peace be upon Israel!"* **(Psalm 128:1-6).**

> *"¹Praise the Lord!* **Blessed is the man who fears the Lord,** *who delights greatly in His commandments.²***His descendants will be mighty on earth; the generation of the upright will be blessed.** *³Wealth*

and riches will be in his house, and his righteousness endures forever" **(Psalm 112:1-3).**

YOU ARE DIFFERENT BECAUSE YOU ARE FAVORED

His love saved you; His favor differentiates you. You are blessed and highly favored. There is a difference between God's people and the people of the world. God's people are separate; different, peculiar, holy and empowered to live. That is what Israel means; "one who has power with God." And God does make a difference between His people and the people of the world.

There is a difference between God's people and the people of the world.

"Then you shall again discern between the righteous and the wicked, between one who serves God and one who does not serve Him" **(Malachi 3:18 KJV).**

CHAPTER 7

COVENANT REALITY

The Reality of Divine Favor on Your Life

THE TRUTH THAT GOD DOES FAVOR HIS PEOPLE

You are blessed and highly favored.

❖ You are different because you are favored.

❖ There is a difference between God's people and the people of the world.

❖ The favor of the Lord is for a lifetime.

❖ The fear of the Lord brings favor.

❖ You already have the favor of God, but great favor you must ask for.

PRAY for:

> **Protecting Favor**
> **Providential Favor**
> **Distinguishing Favor**
> **Exceptional Favor**
> **Favor in Answer to Prayers**
> **Uncommon Favor**
> **Great Favor**

Declarations:
"Let the redeemed of the Lord say so..." (Psalm 107:2).
"You will also decide and decree a thing, and it will be established for you; And the light [of **God's favor**] will shine upon your ways" **(Job 22:28 AMP).**

I declare God's favor over my life, my family, my ministry and all that pertains to me. I declare that I am blessed and highly favored by God; the shield of favor surrounds me. I have the protecting favor of God, therefore, no evil or diseases shall come near me or my dwelling, and my enemies shall not triumph over me.

I declare I am my Father's child; therefore, I shall not lack any good thing His providential favor is upon my life.

I stand out because I am anointed, honored and chosen by my Father. Today I shall receive preferential treatments and special considerations from people wherever I go because God's exceptional favor is at work on my behalf.

I will receive answers to my prayers and prayers for others because God favors me.

I declare a full restoration of everything the devil has stolen from me. I receive great favor today in Jesus Name. I thank you God for your favor is for my lifetime.

Welcome to this Page!

PRAYER TO RECEIVE JESUS

If you have never asked Jesus Christ into your life to be your personal Savior, may I invite you to do so right now. He has already died and redeemed you back to God, but to be saved, you must personally receive Jesus Christ by faith. When you do so, He will save you and deliver you from the power of sin and darkness and bring you into the family of God, and your new life will begin in Him. **Would you say this prayer now?**

"Father, I acknowledge that I am a sinner and my sins have separated me from you. I am truly sorry, and ask for your forgiveness. I believe that Jesus died for my sins, and was raised from the dead, He is alive, and hears my prayers now. I invite Jesus now to come into my heart and be my Lord and Savior, I give my life to Him now. Lord Jesus, please write my name in the Book of Life, I commit my future in to your hands. And thank you for the gift of salvation. In Jesus Name I pray, Amen."

If you have said this prayer, congratulations! You have made the best decision of your life. You are now a child of God. So what's next? You are a new babe in Christ, and you will need to pay attention to certain things that will help you grow to become mature in Christ (a disciple). Also to have fellowship (time together) with other Bible believing Christians in a Church that truly teaches the Bible so you can learn the Word of God. These will help you grow and realize the joy of knowing Jesus. Should you have any questions or like to share your decision today, please write to the address below:

Michael Atunrase, Sr.
MOLAT PUBLISHERS
P. O. Box 82
Morrisville, PA 19067 U.S.A.
7Realitiesdaily@gmail.com

SCRIPTURE INDEX

Introduction
Proverbs 19:2 AMP
Matthew 14:35
John 4:15
John 6:34 KJV
1 Corinthians 2:12 NLT
Hosea 4:6a
Isaiah 5:13
2 Corinthians 2:11
Luke 19:42 ISV
Ephesians 1:18 NIV
Genesis 47:27 NIV
Exodus 1:7-10
Isaiah 54:17
Acts 7:17 NIV
Psalm 105:24 NIV
1 Chronicles 27:23 NIV
Genesis 12:2 NIV
Genesis 15:5
Genesis 26:3-4
Genesis 46:3 NIV
Genesis 48:3-4 NIV
Isaiah 5:13
Job 1:9-10
Psalm 34:7
Genesis 48:16
Exodus 6:6
Leviticus 25:47-49
Leviticus 25:25 NIV
Ruth 4:3-4
Romans 6:23
Titus 2:14 KJV
Luke 24:21
1 Peter 1:18-19
Hebrews 9:12 KJV
Galatians 3:13

Galatians 4:4-5 KJV
Exodus 14:30 KJV
1 Samuel 14:6
Isaiah 45:22 KJV
1 Timothy 2:5-6
John 3:16 KJV
Acts 10:43
Galatians 3:22
Romans 5:10 AMPC
2 Peter 1:4
John 3:6
Romans 6:22
2 Corinthians 5:17
Romans 12:2
2 Corinthians 3:18
Romans 5:18
Romans 8:30
John 15:16
Psalm 92:12
Acts 4:12
Luke 19:9
Galatians 3:15-18
Genesis 12:3
Galatians 3:7
Galatians 3:29

Chapter 1
The Reality of Your Redemption Provisions and Covenant Rights

Exodus 6:6
Ephesians 1:7
Isaiah 33:24 NIV
Matthew 9:2

Luke 13:16
John 11:3
Exodus 15:26
Jeremiah 33:6
Jeremiah 30:17
1 John 2:9
1 Peter 2:24
Galatians 4:4-7
Romans 8:17
Revelation 5:12
Acts 26:16-18
Ephesians 2:12

Chapter 2
The Reality of the Superiority of Your Covenant Status

Exodus 1:9
Deuteronomy 32:31 KJV
Isaiah 61:9 MSG
Psalm 105:24
1 John 5:4 NIV
Romans 8:37
2 Chronicles 32:7-8
Romans 8:31
Joshua 2:9-11
Genesis 26:16
Matthew 16:18
Exodus 7:10-12
2 Corinthians 10:4
Exodus 14:25
Psalm 18:32-33
Revelation 1:5-6 NIV
Isaiah 9:7
Daniel 2:44
Matthew 3:1-2
Ephesians 1:20-21, 2:6
Luke 9:1-2

Luke 10:8-9
Matthew 16:19
Ephesians 3:10
Psalms 149:6-9
1 Timothy 2:3-4
Acts 26:16-18
1 John 3:2
1 Timothy 6:17
Matthew 6:10 KJV

Chapter 3
The Reality of Your Spiritual Potential

Exodus 1:10
1 Samuel 13:19, 22 NLT
2 Corinthians 6:1
1 Corinthians 15:10 KJV
Philippians 3:12
Galatians 4:1-5 NIV
Judges 1:28
Ephesians 3:20
Acts 1:8
2 Kings 2:9
John 3:34
1 Samuel 18:5,14,16 NLT
Psalm 37:23
Psalm 78:72
1 Samuel 16:18 MSG
2 Samuel 23:1-2
2 Samuel 17:8 NIV
Proverbs 11:11a
Psalms 22
Psalm 110
2 Peter 3:18
2 Peter 1:5-11
Ephesians 4:13

Chapter 4
The Reality of the Source of All Spiritual Warfare and afflictions

Exodus 1:11 KJV
2 Corinthians 12:7
Acts 10:38
Luke 13:16
3 John 2 KJV

Chapter 5
The Reality of the Benefits of Trials

Exodus 1:12
Psalm 34:19
Hebrews 12:1 KJV
James 1:3
1 Peter 1:7 NLT
Job 23:10
Matthew 16:18 NLT
James 1:2-4, 12
Genesis 50:20
Psalm 119:67
Psalm 119:71
Philippians 1:12
1 Corinthians 10:13
2 Corinthians 4:17
Deuteronomy 8:16 NIV
2 Corinthians 4:17 NLT
2 Corinthians 4:17 Weymouth
Romans 8:28
Romans 8:17
Romans 8:18
1 Peter 4:13 KJV
1 Peter 5:1
1 Corinthians 10:13 BSB

Chapter 6
The Reality of the Remarkable Impact of A Christ-like life.

Exodus 1:12 AMP
Exodus 1:12 KJV
Deuteronomy 2:25
Deuteronomy 11:25
Genesis 35:5
Proverbs 11:11 AMP
Genesis 41:38 MSG
Joshua 11:16-19
Joshua 14:11
1 Kings 18:17
Psalm 101:8 NLT
1 Chronicles 14:16-17
Daniel 5:11 KJV
1 John3:8b
Acts 10:38
Mark 5:7 NLT
John 12:19 AMP
Acts 19:15
Acts 16:20
Acts 17:6
Acts 3:1-10
Acts 4:16 NIV
Romans 8:19
Isaiah 52:1-2
Romans 13:11-12

Chapter 7
The Reality of Divine Favor on Your Life

Exodus 1:19-20 KJV
Psalm 5:12 NIV
Romans 8:11
Deuteronomy 34:7 NLT
Joshua 14:11

Psalm 5:12 NIV

1 Samuel 23:14

1 Samuel 23:25-26

Psalm 71:10-12

1 Samuel 23:27-28

Psalm 27:1-6

2 Corinthians 9:8

Genesis 26:12-14

Exodus 16:35

Genesis 39:2-3

Psalm 89:20-29

1 Kings 4:29-34

Daniel 1:9

Job 1:3

Psalm 89:17

Exodus 8:23

Exodus 9:4,6

Deuteronomy 4:34 NIV

2 Samuel 7:23 NIV

Psalm 106:46 NIV

Isaiah 14:1 NLT

Deuteronomy 33:29 NIV

Exodus 19:5 NIV

Luke 4:25-26

Luke 4:27

Luke 1:28

2 Chronicles 7:14 KJV

Job 22:28 AMP

Isaiah 65:24 KJV

Joshua 10:12-14 NLT

Esther 2:9,10, 15, 17

Ephesians 2:4-6

John 1:16 NLT

1 Kings 11:19

Psalm 30:5 AMP

Lamentations 3:22-23

Jeremiah 32:40 NLT

Daniel 11:32

Proverbs 29:25

Proverbs 28:14 AMP

Proverbs 16:7

Psalm 128:1-6

Psalm 112:1-3

Malachi 3:18 KJV

ABOUT THE AUTHOR

 **MICHAEL O. ATUNRASE, SR. Ph.D.,** is Senior Pastor of Cornerstone Bible Fellowship Church, Levittown, Pennsylvania. His unique way of sharing profound truths is aimed at bringing unbelievers to Christ, and aiding believers toward Christian growth and increasing commitment to Christ. Pastor Atunrase's teaching ministry animates real life with real hope. His depth of spiritual insight and honest reflections about life inspire people around the world to faith, hope, love and joy. His teachings necessitate a disciplined study of the word of God. A visionary and a missionary, he has traveled extensively, preaching and lecturing in several countries, and has studied and demonstrated proficiency in various fields such as Theology, Education, Christian Counseling, Writing, Speaking and Applied Sciences, (Biochemistry, Bacteriology and Public Health). Dr. Atunrase is author of online daily devotions, 'Daily Refreshing', and President of MOVE-MENt, an International Ministry to Men. He is President of Cornerstone International Christian Ministries and Protestant Minister, for the State of New Jersey, Department of Rehabilitation and is an ordained Bishop with the Association of the Evangelical Gospel Assemblies, USA. He is blessed with his wife Pastor Lola and their four children, Michael Jr., Emily, Sarah and Joshua.

For information on speaking, seminars and workshops, contact Dr. Michael Atunrase, Sr. at

MOLAT PUBLISHERS
P.O Box 82,
Morrisville, PA 19067
Email:7Realitiesdaily@gmail.com

Helping Pastors Who Disciple Men
Have A Men's Group? We can Help.

Your Men are in for a wonderful encounter with God at a MOVE-MEN† Weekend Retreat.

CONTACT US NOW FOR YOUR NEXT
Men's Outreach Program.
movementretreats@gmail.com

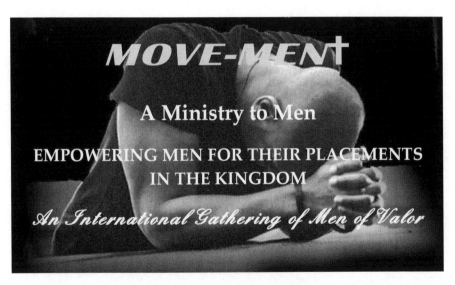

The Mission of MOVE-MENT

The MOVE-MENT is an international ministry aimed at empowering Men for their placements in the Kingdom, by providing Leadership, Mentoring, Discipleship, Fellowship, Ministry, Networking, Peering, and opportunity for Global Missions. It is a ministry for men with hearts after God who desire to merge action with passion in their pursuit of a closer walk with God. The ministry is designed to promote fellowship among godly men and to encourage them in their Journey of Biblical Manhood.

Notes

Notes

Notes

59956689R00076

Made in the USA
Charleston, SC
21 August 2016